W9-CCB-598

Julaine Kammrath

Laugh & Tickle, Hug & Pray

active family devotions

CPH.
SAINT LOUIS

Scripture quotations marked KJV are from the King James or Authorized Version of the Bible.

All Scripture quotations, unless otherwise indicated, are taken from the HOLY BIBLE, NEW INTERNATIONAL VERSION®. NIV®. Copyright © 1973, 1978, 1984 by International Bible Society. Used by permission of Zondervan Publishing House. All rights reserved.

All hymn references are taken from *Lutheran Worship*, copyright © 1982 by Concordia Publishing House. All rights reserved.

Text for "Our Father, by Whose Name" © The Church Pension Fund. Used by permission.

Text for "Lift Up Your Head, You Mighty Gates" © Concordia Publishing House. All rights reserved.

Copyright © 1997 Concordia Publishing House
3558 S. Jefferson Avenue, St. Louis, MO 63118-3968
Manufactured in the United States of America

Parents or other individuals who purchase this product may reproduce pages as needed for in-home completion of activities.

All rights reserved. Except as noted above no part of this publication may be reproduced, stored in a retrieval system, or transmitted, in any form or by any means, electronic, mechanical, photocopying, recording, or otherwise, without the prior written permission of Concordia Publishing House.

Library of Congress Cataloging-in-Publication Data

Kammrath, Julaine.
    Laugh and tickle, hug and pray : active family devotions / Julaine Kammrath.
      p.   cm.
    ISBN 0-570-04991-1
    1. Family—Prayer-books and devotions—English.   2. Children—Prayer-books and devotions—English.   3. Christian education—Activity programs.   4. Christian education—Home training.   5. Christian education of children.   6. Lutheran Church—Missouri Synod—Prayer-books and devotions—English.   I. Title.
    BV4526.2.K36   1997
    249—dc21   97-10414

    3   4   5   6   7   8   9   10   06   05   04   03   02   01   00   99   98

 **To my husband,
25 years on the same road**

Contents

Special Times

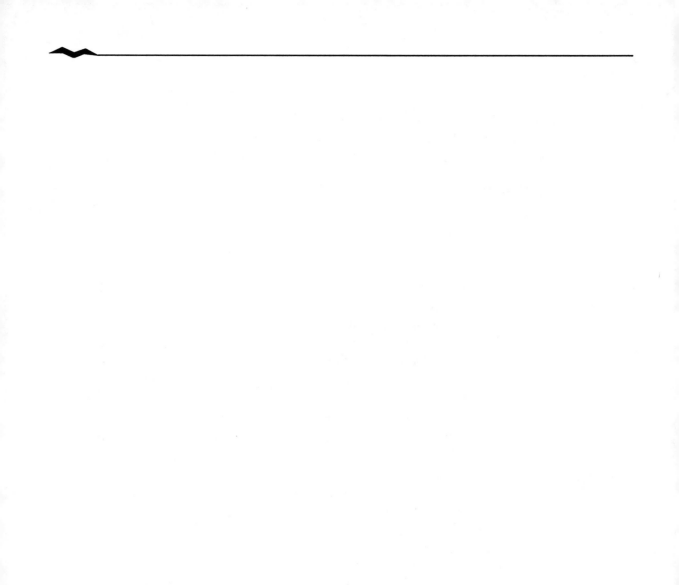

Introduction

My son leaves home for college this year. His childhood is over. What will he remember? Will he miss us and the things we did together? Will he eagerly return next summer? Will he stay close to God?

A neighbor—a mother of five—once told me, "Your children are like investments. What you put in now will pay dividends later." How can we intentionally invest love into our family? How can we draw near to the Source of all love?

God gave us the model immediately after He created us! He calls it "Sabbath rest." He made it for us—one day out of the week when work is balanced with refreshment and reflection. For many of us, that day is Sunday. For others, it may fall on a different day. No matter what, God has taught us to set aside time from our busy lives to reflect, to pray, and to hear His Word and the Good News that His Son died for us!

Why do we need this time? We need it in order to

- look thoughtfully into each other's eyes;
- listen deeply;
- speak of what really matters;
- laugh and tickle, hug and pray; and
- reflect on God's perfect love for us.

When we started our family, there were no books on how to invite God into our lives. So we talked to people who seemed to have figured it out. We searched the Bible for traditions we could adapt. The goal was to invite God into our family and then join hands with Him. Many of our family's traditions and activities are in this book—as well as many we wish we had done!

Years from now, when our son brings our grandchildren to the Thanksgiving table, will he look for the Indian corn blessing? Will he reminisce with his sisters about the year the Easter lamb cake fell all over the oven? Will he confidently pray aloud after the meal? Will he bring his children around the piano for our regular songfest? I think so. "Train a child in the way he should go, and when he is old he will not turn from it" (Proverbs 22:6).

May God bless your family! May He come close to those you love the most! May you and your love grow stronger in Him and may your family stand whole and together in Christ.

Note: It might be wise to look ahead before each family time to prepare materials should you decide to do a suggested craft or game. Intersperse the suggested special holiday family times with the regular family times.

Regular Times
Regular Times
Regular Times
Regular Times
Regular Times
Regular Times
Regular Times

God Is Good

Stop and Think

I heard a sharp rap on the door. Gavin, a 6'6"-tall high school senior, came in. "Mrs. K., do you know anything about birds?"

"Well, I used to raise finches. What do you want to know?"

"We found a little bird, about this big." Gavin held his hands about three inches apart. "It tried to hop away from us, but it couldn't fly. Maybe it's sick."

"Maybe it's a baby that fell out of its nest," I suggested.

"Well—whatever, we put it in Miss Jennings' science room."

We left my house and walked next door to the school. The baby bird sat in a broken fish tank, protected from the jagged glass by a sheet of cardboard.

I saw baby fuzz around the bird's eyes and sides. It might be a baby sparrow, I thought. The bird stood stock still, beak facing upward, and little chest heaving.

"Did you phone your teacher, Miss Jennings?" I asked Gavin.

"Yes, she wasn't home," he answered as we both knelt beside the cage. "Will you take it home, Mrs. K.?"

I sighed. "I suppose we'll find a spot. It probably needs water. Hopefully Miss Jennings will know how to feed it tomorrow."

Gavin and I made a cardboard lid for the tank. Gavin carried it to our house. He set it on the kitchen counter, almost tripping over Wizzy, our cat. Hmm, I thought. Better move the cat.

"Barbara!" I called. "Please come and help!"

My daughter, Barbara, left her homework and came running to see the little bird. "Can you take Wizzy?" I asked.

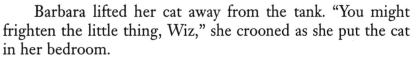

Barbara lifted her cat away from the tank. "You might frighten the little thing, Wiz," she crooned as she put the cat in her bedroom.

Then she came back and asked, "What can I do to help?"

"Look in the junk drawer for an eye dropper while I get some lukewarm water." Barbara carefully lifted the cardboard lid while I began dropping water on the baby's beak.

It stood there stoically, staring straight up, beak closed tight. "Tap on its beak a bit, Mom—maybe try the side," said Barbara.

So I tapped on the side of the baby's beak. Suddenly its little mouth opened and the drops rolled down. Its little eyes closed as it drank and drank.

Jesus once said, "Are not two sparrows sold for a penny? Yet not one of them will fall to the ground apart from the will of your Father" (Matthew 10:29). God decided that this little sparrow would be cared for by many people: Gavin, Barbara, Miss Jennings, and me. Four people for one baby bird! That's how good God is!

Look and Listen

Read a different story Jesus told in Luke 10:30–37. To what city was the man going? Which people were not good to the man? Why? What did the Samaritan do? Why? Who did Jesus say was the good neighbor?

Now read something that really happened in Luke 19:1–9. In what city was Zacchaeus? Which people were not good to Zacchaeus? Why? What did Jesus do? Why? Who do you think was the good neighbor?

Some people from China believe in *yin-yang*. This term refers to the balance of opposites. So, for example, they eat something sweet and something sour in a meal. They also believe in good gods and evil gods. Imagine how they fear those evil gods! What a blessing you have knowing Jesus is the one true God!

How is God good to us in the most important way? Right—He sent His Son to die for us to take the punishment for our sins. God is good to us in other ways too. Think about your environment, inside and outside. Name sights, sounds, smells, touches, and tastes that are good. Now think about the people God has put in your life at home, in the neighborhood, at church, at school, and on the other end of the phone. Name them. What about activities that you enjoy? Name some of those. There are even good things we can't see with our eyes like our consciences, music, and sleep! God is very, very good!

God sighting. Have each person in your family make a "God is good" note and tape it so that it hangs from an inside shelf of the refrigerator. As family members experience God's goodness during the week, they may each move their note to the outside of the refrigerator and share what God has done for them.

Proceed with Care

✔ Celebrate God's goodness in giving you a comfortable home. Eat in a different room every night this week. Consider novel ideas, such as eating under a "tent" made of bed sheets in your child's room; turning up the heat, putting on shorts, and having a picnic in the living room; changing your bedroom into a French restaurant; or decorating the bathroom like a railroad diner. Plan menus and a dinner conversation question.

✔ Play I Spy. The object of the game is to guess within three clues what the player has targeted. Play this game anywhere—the car, the doctor's office, or the grocery store checkout lane. Your child might say, "I spy something black." You guess the black cover on your steering wheel. If that was a wrong guess, your child says, "I spy something black and small." You guess the handle of the glove box compartment. You got it right. Your turn!

- Make apple butter and thank God for giving us good things to taste. Quarter and peel five pounds of apples. Mix with 1 cup white wine vinegar, 1½ cups honey, ¼ teaspoon salt, 2 teaspoons cinnamon, 1 teaspoon cloves, and 2 tablespoons lemon juice. Cook on medium heat, covered, for 15 minutes. Then uncover and stir until mushy.

- Challenge each family member to bring back four treasures in the next 10 minutes: something old but good, something new and good, something of great value to me, something God has given me.

- Children don't often think of their bodies as good gifts from God. Try this demonstration to discover a little-known way your body works: Have one person sit in a chair with a finger gently plugging one ear. Then have someone else stand behind her and tap two spoons together behind either the right or left ear. Ask her if she can tell which ear the tap was closest to. Try it several times. (We need both ears to help us locate sound. One ear will perceive the sound as louder than the other, which helps us know where the sound came from.) Here's another experiment: Can you eat standing on your head? Have someone try it. (Yes, we can. The esophagus is not a pipe like our windpipe. It is a series of ring-like muscles that squeeze in succession when food is headed for the stomach.) Here's one more: Use an encyclopedia to look up "human body." Then write the names of the major bones on slips of paper. Let the kids tape the paper slips onto Dad or Mom at the correct location.

Read God's Word to us in Psalm 103:2–5. Then substitute each of your names in the verse in the appropriate places: "Praise the LORD, *Gavin*, and forget not all His benefits—who forgives all *Gavin's* sins and heals all *his* diseases, who redeems *Gavin's* life from the pit and crowns *him* with love and compassion, who satisfies *Gavin's* desires with good things." Then thank God that these words are true.

Go in Peace

God Is Wise

Stop and Think

If you've ever seen a movie about Jesus' life, the soldiers in armor and helmets were the Romans. Most Romans believed in false gods like Jupiter, who threw lightning bolts; or Mercury, who delivered mail between the people and the gods. One god, Janus, had two heads, one facing backward and one facing forward. Those heads were supposed to help him see the past and the future at the same time. The month January is named after Janus.

You and I cannot see the future. We only know what is happening right now in our lives and sometimes in the lives of others. Do you know what is happening at this moment in the life of someone in another city? Ten years from now, will you know everything that has happened to this person? No! No one, not even angels, can see the past, present, and future of everyone. Only God can do that.

Even if we could see everything in the past, present, and future, could we work all the details out so that every bad event would be turned into something good for us?

Imagine that in front of you is a 3-D layout of a city. On

it are 2,000 Matchbox-size cars, all moving. Now, even though your layout has stoplights and stop signs, the cars sometimes go through intersections without stopping. You can make trees fall across the road, cars run out of gas, or police cars move into an area. Can you keep track of all 2,000 cars so there are no accidents?

How many people do you guess are in the world? How many of those people break God's rules? How many people does God keep track of?

God keeps track of everything that exists—every plant, animal, mountain, stream, gas, and star! God's job is much bigger than those 2,000 cars! Paul knew this when he wrote his letter to the Romans:

> *Oh, the depth of the riches of the wisdom and knowledge of God! How unsearchable His judgments, and His paths beyond tracing out! "Who has known the mind of the Lord? Or who has been His counselor? Who has ever given to God that God should repay him?" For from Him and through Him and to Him are all things. To Him be the glory forever! Amen (Romans 11:33–36).*

God is wise. He has made so many incredible things; even scientists can't figure them out. Why do you think God puts these amazing things before us?

Look and Listen

The Bible tells us that on the third day—Sunday—after Jesus was crucified, two men were walking toward Emmaus, a town near Jerusalem. As they walked, Jesus joined them, but they didn't recognize Him. They discussed the strange happenings in Jerusalem—angels telling some women, "Jesus is alive." This story from the women didn't make sense. The two men had believed the Messiah would overthrow the Roman soldiers and become a Jewish king like King David. Here was a man who could walk on water, talk to a storm, multiply bread, cure people, turn water to wine, and even make dead people alive again! How could Jesus have allowed the Romans to kill Him? Jesus spoke up. He reminded the men of the many prophecies about Him that said He had to die in order to save us. This story is found in Luke 24:13–35 if you want to find out what happened next.

Jesus knew He would be killed. He forewarned His disciples many times before that Friday. Jesus could see and understand the past and the future, and He knew His death would affect everything else. Jesus is wise.

God sighting. If you see a colony of ants or a hive of bees this week, remember that God knows what each of these tiny creatures is doing, has done, and will do. Think about how many ants and bees exist in the world! God knows what is best for you!

Proceed with Care

- ✔ Play this word association game. Have a person in your family say each of the following words. The other family members name the first person that comes to mind. Don't allow a lot of time for thinking. The goal is to get the first response from each person. Here's the list: *fun to be with, silly, famous, full of kindness, villain, hero, pretty, athletic, singer, patient, wise.*

- ✔ Make a honey treat together to remind you of this week's "God sighting": Mix ¼ cup softened butter or margarine, ½ cup honey, ½ cup coconut flakes, and ½ cup nuts. Spread the ingredients on a 9″ cake you have already baked. Broil until the topping is bubbly.

- ✔ Mix 4 tablespoons baking soda in a cup. Then add ¼ cup vinegar. Can you explain why the mixture bubbles? Chemists can explain it now, but people in Jesus' day could not. God understands how the molecules work in everything!

- ✔ Play a cause-and-effect game. Sit in a circle and designate a starter who says, "Because ... " Each person in turn says, "Therefore ..." For example: "Because the toy was left out ..." "Therefore the little girl cried." You can substitute "since" for "because" and "so" or "and" for "therefore." Try to use examples from the Bible: "Because the people in Noah's day displeased God ..." "Therefore ... ." "Because God loves us ..." "Therefore ... ." What other example of cause and effect can you find?

- ✔ Make some "Wise Words" cards. Copy these phrases onto index cards: *I'm sorry. Thank you; that was kind. It was my fault. I would like a turn now, please. Let's look at this another way. Maybe you're right; I'll think about it. Let's stop because we're getting upset. I need some time to myself right now.* Show each card to the family and discuss situations where these might be wise words.

- ✔ Finish this poem:

  > Look, God's fingerprints on me.
  > Dust my head, and you will see
  > Marks of ___ ___ ___ ___ ___

Go in Peace

Take out a local area map or find your state in an atlas. Count all the cities in your area. Each family member can choose a city by name. Then talk to God about His care for the people in that city. Consider praying in gratitude for the greatest blessing we can have, knowing Him. Pray also that He will clean the hearts and renew the minds of the people in those cities so they can powerfully witness for Him.

Jesus Is the Truth

Jolina huddled inside her closet. When Mama found out, Jolina would be in for it. "Everything is always my fault," she told herself. "No matter how hard I try, I always mess up. I'm only important when I make other people happy. And Mama's not happy."

A tear slipped down Jolina's cheek as she pulled her skinny knees closer to her chest. She heard the phone ring.

"I wish I could be like Bradley. He's so smart and everybody likes him at school. Even Mr. Krempler, the principal, likes him."

Jolina heard Mama's footsteps. She tried not to breathe. The footsteps came closer, then she heard a hand grip the doorknob. Light flooded the dark corner where Jolina had scrunched, head on knees.

"Jolina, you come on out of there," said Mama.

Mama stepped aside to let Jolina out. "Honey, sit down over there." Jolina shuffled over to her bed, staring down at her feet.

"Jolina, Mr. Krempler just called. He said one of the kids at school saw you take Bradley's calculator. You've been talking about that calculator till we're all tired of hearing about it. Did you take it?"

Jolina struggled with her answer. The calculator was hidden in her secret hiding place—the farthest corner under the bed. What would Mama do if she told her the truth? "No," she faltered.

"Jolina," Mama's voice was soft. "You know that when we let a lie into our hearts, it sits there like a piece of ugly gray mold. Pretty soon we tell more lies to cover up the first lie. Next thing you know, that little piece of mold is covering up more and more of our hearts. Look at me, Jolina. I love you. I want you to be clean inside."

Jolina looked at her mother's face. The wrinkles around Mama's eyes were smiling even though her eyes were serious. "Mama, I try so hard in math at school, but I never get A's. If I could have a calculator like Bradley's, I'd get good grades, and people would like me. The way I am, I'm not very important to anybody. I'm always messing up."

Mama sat down on the bed next to Jolina and began stroking her hair. "It's true you certainly are the dickens sometimes. You often don't think before you go tearing into something. You're learning, though. And God has made you with so many wonderful parts, Jolina. Who makes the baby laugh when he's fussy? Who is quick to welcome visitors and make them enjoy our home? Who reads stories to your little sister when I'm busy? You have very quick eyes, Jolina, and God certainly has put lots of kindness in your soul. I'd say you are very important."

Jolina leaned against her mother and said, "I took the calculator. I'm very sorry. I know that taking it was wrong. I'll give it back to Bradley as soon as I've told God I'm sorry. I want to ask Him to clean that ugly lie off my heart."

Look and Listen

The Bible tells us that Satan is a liar. He whispers lies into our minds and then makes us think they are true. That way he can make us slaves to fear and sadness and anger. Read John 8:31–34.

What is a slave? (Slaves can't get away. They have to do whatever their owner tells them to do.) If we are slaves to a sin like lying, then we will obey inside urges to lie. The more we lie, the more lying grows in our hearts. Jesus sets us free from that sin. Jesus is the truth. He cleans out the ugly lie spot. He helps us fight the pattern of lying. That place in our hearts is "sanctified" by Christ (John 17:17).

God's truth also protects us from troubles. Read Psalm 40:11–12. When we know Jesus is standing in our hearts as the truth, we recognize the lies other people tell us—lies like: "Go ahead, nobody will see" or "Everybody else does it so you can too." Have you ever heard lies like that?

Did you know that "I tell you the truth" was something Jesus said time and time again? Matthew recorded Him saying those words 30 times. Jesus said, "I am the way, the truth, and the life" (John 14:6). He meant that He is the way to God now and in heaven; He is the truth who frees us from Satan's lies; and He is the giver of abundant, overflowing life.

God sighting. Have you believed anyone who said, "Do what's best for you—others aren't your concern," even though you knew it was a lie? Ask Jesus to forgive you and to sanctify that place in your heart.

Proceed with Care

- ✔ Avoiding sin can seem like an obstacle course. Set up your own obstacle course! Crawl through a box, jump over a rope, hop through the holes in a ladder on the floor, balance a Ping-Pong ball on a spoon while going up and down a step stool, toss a ball off the wall and catch it, and squirm under chairs. Give prizes and help the kids make the course more challenging.

- ✔ Make papier-mâché masks. Mix ½ cup flour with ¼ cup cold water. Gradually add 1 cup very hot water until the consistency is like a cream soup. Soak ½" newspaper strips in this mixture. Lay the strips in several layers on one side of a blown-up balloon. Shape the strips to make a nose. Allow to dry. Pop the balloon and cut out eye and mouth holes. Paint. If you have the time, look for a book on masks in your children's library. Talk together about the masks people hide behind because they don't want to show that they may be afraid or upset. Jesus always showed His true self whether He was happy, angry, or sad.

✔ In China, honey is smeared on the kitchen idol's lips so that during its annual report to the "god of heaven" it will say nice things about the family. What does this tell you about how smart these idol worshipers believe the "god of heaven" to be? In Genesis 4, who tried to trick God? Other people tried to lie to God in Joshua 7:10–26 and Acts 5:1–10. What do you think the people who tried to lie to God thought about Him?

Go in Peace

On heart-shaped paper, write down a lie you have told. Pour bleach and water into a red bucket or into a cup covered with red paper. Say, "Jesus' blood cleanses us from all sin." Dip your lies into the liquid and notice that sins are cleaned away. This is what Jesus' blood does for our real sins.

God Is Just

Stop and Think

"You can't tell me what to do! I can do whatever I want!" Steve stomped out of the kindergarten classroom and slammed the door. After a stunned silence, everyone in the room began to chatter.

Mrs. Mullins, the kindergarten teacher, called Carlan to her desk. "Please take this note down to the principal." Then she hurried from the room. Carlan ran to the office as the rest of the class gathered at the windows that faced the playground. They could see Mrs. Mullins heading for Steve, who was throwing rocks at the building. When Steve saw her, he took the rock in his hand and threw it at her.

Mrs. Mullins dodged the rock. Steve threw another one and hit her in the leg. The children were shocked at this new outrage. Since the new student, Steve, had entered their class this morning, he'd dumped paint, grabbed toys from others, kicked the chair in the time-out corner, and tripped the helper carrying the juice. But this last act was beyond "naughty."

As Mr. Justin came around the corner of the building, Steve turned to run out the front gates to the playground. But before Steve had gotten more than a few steps, Mr. Justin's strong arms were around him. Steve pulled back his foot to kick Mr. Justin's shin, but the principal was quicker. He held Steve tight so that his feet couldn't kick. Mrs. Mullins and Mr. Justin walked back toward the building, both quietly talking to a crying Steve.

The children crowded around their teacher as she entered the room, but they quickly sat on the floor where she pointed. "Let's talk about this," she said.

What would you have wanted to say?

Look and Listen

In Genesis there were two people who treated God like Steve treated his teacher. God had given them only one special rule. He said, "You are free to eat from any tree in the garden but you must not eat from the tree of the knowledge of good and evil" (Genesis 2:16–17). So the two people ate of all the many other trees: apples, pears, cherries, and even a tree no one else on our earth has ever seen—the tree of life. They talked with God often and asked Him about choices. They believed and trusted God and talked everything over with Him.

But their wonderful lives changed one day when Satan, disguised as a serpent, convinced the woman she'd be better off if she could decide everything for herself. Then she wouldn't need God anymore. If she ate the fruit of the tree of the knowledge of good and evil, she'd be like Him—an equal instead of someone under Him. So the woman ate the fruit and gave some to the man, who also ate it. The woman and the man broke God's only rule.

When God came to talk with them like He always did, they hid! God asked them what they had done, and they began blaming the serpent and each other as if what they'd done was not really their fault. But God is just. He punished them for breaking His rules. He sent them away from their beautiful home, and much later, death came to Adam and Eve.

Lots of times we act like Adam or Eve. We say, "Mommy can't tell me what to do! I'll do what she told me not to do!" or "Daddy doesn't know as much as I do, so I'm not going to do what he told me." We decide, "So what if You don't want me to take what isn't mine, God. I need it, so I'm going to take it." Or we think, "I know God says 'Don't lie,' but if I tell the truth, I'll get in trouble." We break God's rules. Sometimes people think that doing good things balances out breaking the rules. But that's not true. A lie is a lie. A sin is a sin. We can't erase our sins ourselves. The punishment for sin is death— away from God's love.

But God is not only just, He is also full of surprising grace. He put the full measure of death—separation from life, love, and Himself—onto Jesus. Those who say, "I believe in Jesus as my Savior from the death I deserve because I break God's rules," are given a PUNISHMENT PAID record in the heavenly justice book. Because of Jesus' love our death on earth is now a door into heaven. God is just *and* He is full of grace.

Can someone *buy* the PUNISHMENT PAID record? Can someone get it by doing good things? No. Only Jesus' death in our place pays for our sins. God is just. He does what He says.

God sighting. Crosses everywhere remind us that we need Jesus as our Savior. We see cross shapes or patterns in flowers, telephone poles, ambulance markers, necklaces, and more. Notice the crosses around you this week.

Proceed with Care

✔ No one since Adam and Eve has ever seen that tree of life because God put an angel with a flaming sword in front of it. But every Christian will see it someday! Read the description in Revelation 22:2 and draw what you think the tree looks like.

✔ Many churches' stained-glass windows have crosses in them. Cut an arch out of typing paper and draw a cross outline on the paper. Then draw five to seven crisscrossing lines over the entire paper to get diamond shapes. Firmly color all the pencil marks with black crayon. Then use markers to color in all the diamonds. Use tissue to rub a little vegetable oil over the entire picture. Let dry. The picture will now be transparent and ready to hang up in a sunny window.

✔ Draw a cross on a cardboard box and let children punch around the shape with a big nail. (Good for small motor strength.)

✔ Make a one-way maze out of cardboard tubes from wrapping paper and toilet tissue paper. Notice from the illustration that some of the tubes are cut in half. Design your own maze. Try to create false paths so the player has to go back and find the correct way out of the maze! Use this game to remind your child that there is only one way to heaven—Jesus!

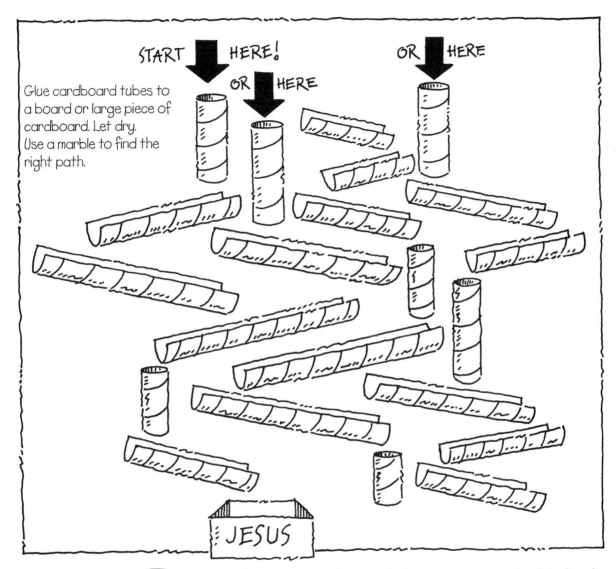

START HERE! OR HERE OR HERE

Glue cardboard tubes to a board or large piece of cardboard. Let dry. Use a marble to find the right path.

JESUS

Go in Peace

What thoughts did you feel were important in this family time? Write them down or tell someone. Then turn those thoughts into prayer. You might begin recording these family prayers in a family journal. This is a record that will give you much pleasure when the children are grown.

God Shares about Sin—Hitting

Mother edged herself down onto the floor beside Brandon. She wondered if she'd be able to get up again. Eight months has definitely made me "great with child," she thought wryly. She could still hear Brandon's little sister sniffing in the next room.

Stop and Think

Brandon's legs stuck out straight but still only just reached past Mom's knee. He was rather short for a first-grader. Mom asked gently, "Brandon, what do you think I'm going to say to you?"

"Don't hit your sister," Brandon singsonged.

I think we need a different approach here, thought Mom. She put her hand over Brandon's. "Can I tell you a story?" Brandon didn't answer, so Mom went on.

"There was once a city where whenever someone was mad, he would hit another person. Pretty soon, stores sold padded clothes—sort of like Pampers jumpsuits. These clothes sold really well during the winter, and people began to be happier and less afraid. Even though the hitting continued, it didn't hurt so much. But as summer arrived, the padded suits got pretty uncomfortable.

"Inventors tried to come up with helpful ideas. One was a clear Plexiglas box made to fit over your body. The TV commercial showed punches bouncing off the suit while the protected person smiled inside. Still, it was difficult walking with the box over your knees.

"Of course, some people carried the old standby, 'Spray Away.' This stuff smelled so horrible that one spray and the hitter would run off. But the person still got punched before he or she had time to find the can.

"There seemed no perfect solution about this hitting

problem until a boy about your age stood up at the Fourth of July concert and said, 'I have an idea.' "

"Can you guess what his idea was, Brandon?"

What do you think Brandon answered?

Look and Listen

God commands us, "Do not kill." Jesus explained this commandment in Matthew 5:39–42. Read this together.

King David often said that the Ten Commandments are a precious gift. They help us understand how we tick. Since God made us, He knows what works for us and what doesn't. Killing and hitting don't work. When I hurt someone on purpose because I'm angry, I break one of God's rules. I am also disrespecting the body of someone God very carefully made. I assume that my anger is more important than the other person's body. The more I hit, the more I turn into a bully. Bullies don't value or respect others. But God is strong enough to punish without turning into a bully.

When we practice the piano or trumpet, we play better. When we practice sports or dancing, we get faster and stronger. When we practice sinning, that behavior gets stronger too. People who yell or hit whenever they get mad soon develop bad tempers. They get angry faster than people who have learned not to get violent.

Brandon's anger hurt both his mom and his sister. Telling his sister, "I'm sorry for hitting. Please forgive me," will help Brandon. But Brandon also can ask Jesus to help him take control of his anger. He can pray whenever he feels the tightness rising in his chest. He can learn to say, "When you move my stuff (or whatever the problem is), I get very, very angry," instead of showing his anger. He can learn to take turns: "You take the first 10 minutes, and then I'll take the next 10. Okay?" He can even learn to walk away from a tense situation.

God sighting. Do you know someone who struggles with yelling, hitting, or kicking in anger? Ask God to help that person control his or her anger. Then see what happens.

Proceed with Care

✔ The pretzel was originally shaped to show a monk with his arms crossed and tucked into the opposite sleeves of his robe. This posture shows a peaceful character with no chance for hitting. Make pretzels by rolling out dough into pencil-sized ropes. Shape them as illustrated.

Dough recipe. Cream ¼ cup margarine with 2 egg yolks. Beat the 2 egg whites, and then fold into the mixture. Mix in 1 cup flour. Roll and shape. Brush with milk and sprinkle with coarse salt. Bake at 375 degrees for 10 minutes.

✔ Rub your hands together fast and hard. Did they get hot? Why? Friction happens between people too. What situations cause friction at your house? What happens during the "hot" exchanges? How did you get your hands to cool off? (You separated them.) Read Proverbs 15:1. Come up with a signal for each other when tempers get too hot.

✔ Trace around your dominant hand on paper and cut out the outline. Glue soft things like cotton balls, flannel, flower petals, marshmallows, and fake fur to it. Now trace around the other hand and cut out that outline. Glue rough things like nails, sandpaper, splinters of wood, and rocks to it. Which hand would you want to tuck you into bed, help you when you are sick, or hold you when you are scared? Why is it important that our hands are gentle?

Go in Peace

Write the word *gentle* on your family members' dominant hands, palm and back. Then ask God to make that hand gentle. Renew the writing as needed this week.

God Shares about Sin— Taking His Name in Vain

Stop and Think

Minh Lee knew that the school planned to honor him at the closing assembly. But he didn't want to hear his name from any of these people ever again. When his mom picked him up on his last day of school, he got into the car without looking back.

It hadn't started that way. His family moved into a neighborhood where all the kids walked to Wilson Elementary School. Everyone seemed friendly, and Minh's eyes shone as he marched with Juan and Neil to first grade. People liked his name, Minh.

He never knew exactly when or how it started. One day he just noticed an odd occurrence—Juan said his name, Minh, without really calling him. He was on the bench for recess baseball when he heard Juan say to Geoffrey, "Oh, Minh, I'll never catch this one!" Later Minh asked what Juan meant. Juan denied ever saying Minh's name.

Not long after that, Minh heard his name again in a similar situation. Neil was looking for his math homework in his desk two rows away. Minh heard, "Minh, my dad's gonna kill me if I get another note from the teacher. I've got to find it! Minh, please let me find it." Minh passed Neil a note saying: "How do you want me to help?" Neil wrote back: "I don't know what you're talking about."

Pretty soon, Minh heard his name several times a day. Even Yuki said, "Minh Lee! She makes me so mad!"

In a few years kids in other grades were saying his name too. One time Minh pulled on Juan's arm and said, "I know you heard that second-grader using my name. You can't say you didn't."

"Yeah, I heard it, but it doesn't mean anything. Everybody says your name. Nobody means anything by it."

"But I never know if someone is trying to talk to me or not! My name is important to me! How would you like it if people were always saying *your* name and not really talking to you!" Minh answered.

"You're being too sensitive," Juan said, breaking away from Minh to join some other kids.

No, I'm not, thought Minh. My name is Minh Lee, and it stands for me. "If someone says my name, it should mean me!" Minh yelled. Juan just turned and gave Minh a puzzled stare.

By fifth grade, Minh even once heard a teacher say, "Minh, Chad, clean out your desk!" Minh didn't bother looking at his own desk. The teacher was pointing at Chad's desk. When Minh's parents said they might move to another state, Minh felt glad.

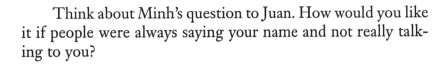

Think about Minh's question to Juan. How would you like it if people were always saying your name and not really talking to you?

Look and Listen

Read James 3:9–12. Can fresh water and salt water come out of the same place? No! The same is true about a person's mouth! People misuse God's name by saying His name when they are not really talking to Him. "God, Susan, can you believe that store clerk!" or "Jesus Christ, get over here right now!" are examples of misusing God's name. Everyone's name is precious. God also never wants us to use His name to curse someone else. When we use God's name to damn someone, we are actually pronouncing judgment for the other person to be in hell eternally! No one has the right to judge except God.

When we use God's name in sin, we deny ourselves three important ways to use His name for good. We can no longer praise God's name in glory from an awestruck heart nor use Jesus' name in power against Satan like Paul did in Acts 16:18. We can never truly pray "in Jesus' name," which is Christ's gift to us as we make requests of God. We can't both misuse and powerfully use God's name—just as salt water and fresh can't come from the same source.

A person who uses God's name in vain probably wonders why worship seems so flat or prayers seem unheard. James tells us: Of course! When you misuse God's name, you're not suddenly going to feel closely connected to Him! Think about it from Minh's point of view. Do you think Minh could have been friends with Juan if Juan didn't misuse Minh's name?

God sighting. Keep track of how many times you hear God's name misused. How many times did you almost misuse it? Pray for guidance to tame your tongue.

↙ Put a piece of glass or clear plastic wrap over any printed surface. Drop one drop of water onto the glass or plastic. The word is magnified! How can we magnify God's name? Use your feet or a shovel to spell "Jesus" in the snow outside, mow "Jesus" in your grass, or print "The Lord our God reigns" on your front door jamb. Have family and friends use light pencils to print favorite names for God on the walls in a soon-to-be painted room, have the kids write "The Lord is my Shepherd" on computer paper and later stencil the words around the top of a bedroom, or shape "Bread of Life" letters out of bread dough and bake for tomorrow's supper.

↙ Create award certificates like "God's Magnifier" for a family member who spoke up for God, "Leader in Righteousness" for someone who championed right over wrong, "Need See-er" for the person who helped with a task without being asked, "Honest under Fire" for the one who told the truth in a difficult situation, or "Persistent" for the person who kept at a frustrating task. Post the awards on that family member's bedroom door.

↙ Pick a three- to five- syllable name for God like "Je-ho-vah" or "Im-man-u-el." Send one person out of the room and give a syllable to each remaining family member. When the person returns, everyone chants his or her syllable out of order. The goal is to guess the name. Suggestions: Redeemer, Counselor, Deliverer, Almighty, Physician, Defender, and Elohim.

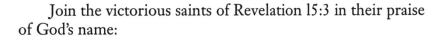

Join the victorious saints of Revelation 15:3 in their praise of God's name:

> Great and marvelous are Your deeds,
>   Lord God Almighty.
> Just and true are Your ways,
>   King of the ages.
> Who will not fear You, O Lord,
>   and bring glory to Your name?
> For You alone are holy.
> All nations will come
>   and worship before You,
> for Your righteous acts have been
>   revealed.

Go in Peace

God Shares about Sin—Stealing

Stop and Think

Brandt pored over the Sears toy catalog. "I wish I could have that ... and that ... and that! I wish I had everything in here. I'd just stay home and play all day."

Mother smiled. "Remember the story we read about Midas, the one who turned everything he touched to gold?"

"Yeah, but I don't want gold. I just want lots of fun stuff," answered Brandt.

"Okay, let's modify the story then. Suppose whatever Midas touched would be his." Mother leaned an elbow on the table.

"You mean Midas could touch the toys in this catalog and they'd be his?" Mother nodded. "Wow! I'd want to be Midas. I'd never have to go to school because I'd never need to get a job! Cool!"

"Maybe. Maybe not. Midas would miss out on a lot," said Mother.

"Miss out? He'd have everything—a mansion, every computer game, TVs in each room, a speed boat, super cars, trips to Disney World, his own swimming pool ... " Brandt was overcome just thinking about it all!

"But he wouldn't know very much. To use the cars and the new computer technology and anything else being invented, Midas would need to keep learning. Otherwise he'd be stuck with only using the old stuff all the rest of his life. He'd also miss the good feeling you get after a job well done, like when you spent all that effort on your science project and got a red ribbon."

"Midas could touch a red ribbon and have it," answered Brandt.

"If I gave you a red ribbon every day, would you feel the same as if you had won one because your project was one of the best in the school?"

"Hmm," Brandt was thinking.

"You know what else Midas would miss—the good feeling of working together with others to accomplish something. For example, when you slam the soccer ball toward your buddy, Miguel, and he sidekicks it into the goal, you and Miguel feel closer. You accomplished something as a team. Midas can't have that by touching things. You can't touch somebody and make him a friend."

Frowning, Brandt put the catalog down on the table. Mother laughed. "I think you're a pretty happy guy, Brandt. You have lots of friends, you have tons of toys, you like school, and you enjoy feeling proud when you work hard. I think you already have more than Midas!"

What do you think—does Brandt have more?

Look and Listen

When you steal, you run the risk of harming someone else and paying for the crime in jail or on probation. Even worse, small stealing done over and over can turn a person into a thief. A thief believes happiness is having things or the money to buy things like vacations and expensive cars. He misses all the other ways God provides pleasures to those He loves. The thief misses seeing how God provides at just the right time. Instead, a thief figures, "This will make me happy, so I'll take it."

That's what a famous but unnamed Jew of Jesus' day must have been thinking. He hated the Roman soldiers who invaded his country and made all sorts of unfair rules. Any time he wanted, a soldier could tell any person to carry something for the soldier a whole mile! How this man must have cursed the Romans! He insulted anyone who didn't curse the Romans too. He even stole from the Romans. Maybe it started with a thought like, "They'll never miss this. They have so much. Besides, they really stole all this stuff from my country, so I'm right to take it back." The more he robbed, the more of a thief he became.

What happened when the man turned into a thief in his heart? Exactly what God told us would happen when He said, "Don't steal." The man lost out on satisfying work, accomplishing something with friends, and knowing he lived for more than eating and buying. He also lost out on trusting God to provide. He missed seeing God surprise him with unexpected gifts.

But God gives amazing grace to those who confess and repent. Read this man's story in Luke 23:32–43. Although there was no time to straighten out the man's life, Jesus did give him the greatest gift of all that no one can steal. What gift was that?

God sighting. What does God do at work, school, or home to help you stay away from stealing? Why does He do that? Watch for any of God's "convictions" this week.

✔ You don't need expensive things to have fun. Use newspapers and tape to create designer clothes for each other. Start with Mom. Give her a hat and jewelry made from newspaper. Then create the next person's outfit. Model it down a "runway" while someone flicks the lights on and off to give a strobe-light effect.

✔ Houses can cost fortunes—unless they're made of old playing cards. Construct some mansions together. See the illustration.

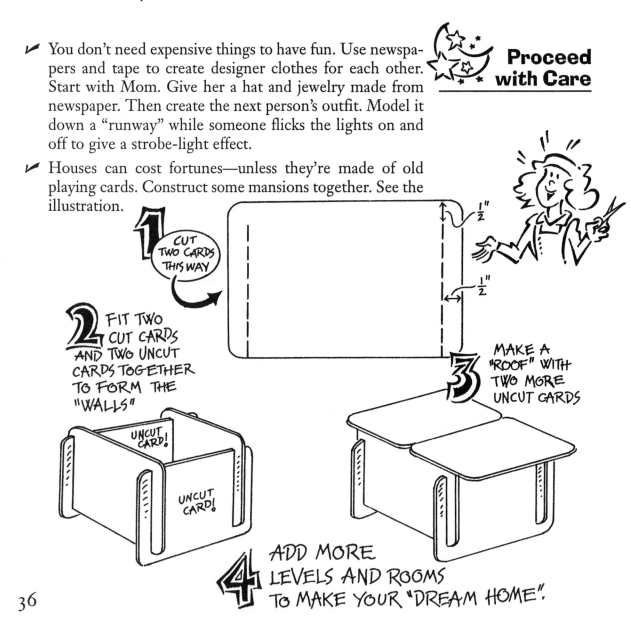

Proceed with Care

1 CUT TWO CARDS THIS WAY

$\frac{1}{2}$"

$\frac{1}{2}$"

2 FIT TWO CUT CARDS AND TWO UNCUT CARDS TOGETHER TO FORM THE "WALLS"

UNCUT CARD!

UNCUT CARD!

3 MAKE A "ROOF" WITH TWO MORE UNCUT CARDS

4 ADD MORE LEVELS AND ROOMS TO MAKE YOUR "DREAM HOME".

- Serve the children breakfast in bed as if they were getting room service in a fancy hotel. (It doesn't have to be morning to do this!) Serve cinnamon toast and tea in fancy cups. Put a flower on the tray. Dress as a valet and put your cheek out for a tip.

- Entertainment doesn't always mean costly floor-show tickets. Host a Family Request Night. "Back by popular demand—Mom, the Incredible!" Each person gets to make a request, such as: Sing 'Row, Row, Row Your Boat' dropping the last word each time"; "Give a one-minute speech on how wonderful Dad is"; "Perform as a circus horse or trained dog"; "Act out all the parts of a fairy tale"; or "Do a soft-shoe dance using a yardstick for a cane." Have fun!

- You too can enjoy the thrill of deep-sea fishing. Cut shark and marlin shapes out of Styrofoam meat trays. Put a metal paper clip on each for a mouth. Tie a string to a magnet and cast off in the bathtub.

Go in Peace

Substitute your names in the following Bible verse in the appropriate places: "[If] *Brandt* has been stealing, *he* must steal no longer but must work, doing something useful with *his* own hands, that *Brandt* may have something to share with those in need" (Ephesians 4:28).

God Shares about Sin—Backbiting

Princess Prunella, surrounded by her ladies-in-waiting, paced her room. "My brother made a fool of himself at the ball, running around with one shoe in his hand. And for what? Some foreigner shows up at the ball and then vanishes. Why, I wouldn't be the least bit surprised if she were an enchanted frog."

"Oh, she was much too pretty to be a magic frog," a lady-in-waiting replied. The others agreed.

Princess Prunella gave the speaker a withering look and lifted her chin. "She wasn't *that* lovely. Her dress was completely out of fashion. My moonstruck brother is behaving as if there weren't dozens of other lovely ladies whirling around the room."

"You certainly stood out in your green gown," crooned another. "You were all loveliness."

The princess halted and looked down her nose. She fluttered her fan and tapped her waist. "I do believe I have the smallest waist of anyone in the kingdom—certainly smaller than that nobody. Only someone with my hair color could have worn that shade of green."

Just then a courier arrived with a proclamation. He stopped abruptly and bowed to the princess and the ladies. "A message from Prince Charming," he read. "The lovely maiden who fits this shoe will be my bride. The shoe may be tried on in the town square." As he dashed away, all the ladies began talking at once. They completely ignored Princess Prunella. Finally, she clomped off, tripping over her rather large feet in disgust.

Look and Listen

Backbiting—saying mean things about people when they aren't around—harms the person who is doing it. Jesus told a parable about a backbiter. Find it in Luke 18:9–14.

Which three types of people did the Pharisee speak against first? Who did he specifically point out? How many times did he tell God and everyone listening how wonderful he was by contrast? What did Jesus say would happen to him (verse 14)?

Can you think of some examples of backbiting or gossiping that you've heard? In every case, the person is giving the message that he or she is better than whoever is being discussed. That's really what Princess Prunella was saying too.

Backbiters eventually lose the ability to see loveliness, kindness, gentleness, and courage in other people. When gossips look at people, they only see weaknesses. God doesn't want this for us. He tells us not to "exalt ourselves" over others. He uses as an example the tax collector who recognized that he was not better than other people. This man's prayer for God's mercy was granted.

Why do you think God lovingly humbles people who act so superior to others? (We can't really recognize how great God is when we're focusing on how wonderful we are.)

God sighting. God is always working to help us become more like Jesus. One way He does this is by using His servants to compliment others when something kind or considerate is done. Pay attention this week for compliments to yourself and to others around you. Don't forget to compliment those around you too!

Proceed with Care

✔ Let your refrigerator be your "building each other up" place. Post school papers, photos of family helpers, compliment phrases, and any family honors (including those for Dad or Mom). Get copies of *Reader's Digest* for older children to read. The section on true-life heroes is always uplifting. Post these stories too!

✔ What happens when you sprinkle pepper on top of a bowl of water? Poke a finger in the water and see what happens. Try a spoon. Now dunk a bar of soap in the water. What happens? How is that bar of soap like God humbling backbiters?

✔ Guess what will happen when you blow air through a card tunnel. Make the tunnel out of a 4″ × 8″ card, folding each short end in one inch. Set it on a table. Can you blow through it and get it off the table? (The moving air has less pressure so the static air over the tunnel pushes down toward the table.) Gossiping is like blowing through the tunnel. Instead of "building others up," which God calls us to do, gossip tries to blow people down. The more we gossip, the more stuck we get!

✔ Find out how stories change when the original goes through many retellings. Play the telephone game—one person whispers a message into the next person's ear. That person then passes it down the line. Ask the last person to repeat what he or she just heard. Is it the same message? Try this variation: The leader draws a picture while the rest close their eyes. Give the original drawing to the next person to redraw. Put the original drawing facedown and mark it "1." Then give the new drawing to the next person who then redraws that picture. Put the second picture facedown and mark it "2." Continue until everyone has drawn the picture. Compare the final picture to the first one. Gossip is almost never as accurate or clear as the original.

✔ This is a good time to get out the fairy tale book and share favorites. Act some of the stories out for one another (maybe videotape them!). Since frogs are in many of the tales, make some out of 5-centimeter × 10-centimeter rectangles. Fold as illustrated.

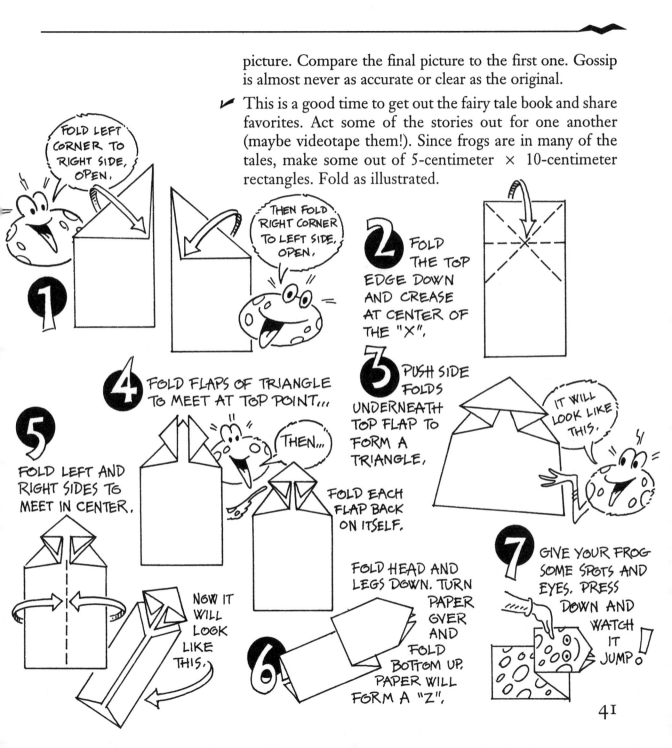

FOLD LEFT CORNER TO RIGHT SIDE, OPEN.

THEN FOLD RIGHT CORNER TO LEFT SIDE, OPEN.

1

2 FOLD THE TOP EDGE DOWN AND CREASE AT CENTER OF THE "X".

4 FOLD FLAPS OF TRIANGLE TO MEET AT TOP POINT....

3 PUSH SIDE FOLDS UNDERNEATH TOP FLAP TO FORM A TRIANGLE.

IT WILL LOOK LIKE THIS.

THEN....

FOLD EACH FLAP BACK ON ITSELF.

5 FOLD LEFT AND RIGHT SIDES TO MEET IN CENTER.

NOW IT WILL LOOK LIKE THIS.

6 FOLD HEAD AND LEGS DOWN. TURN PAPER OVER AND FOLD BOTTOM UP. PAPER WILL FORM A "Z".

7 GIVE YOUR FROG SOME SPOTS AND EYES. PRESS DOWN AND WATCH IT JUMP!

41

Give one to three wooden blocks to each person. (Use books or plastic cups if you don't have blocks.) Think about someone you know who needs God's "building up." As you stack each block, ask God to bless that person with compliments this week. You might ask God if He would help you be one of His builders for a specific person.

Go in Peace

God Shares about Sin— Unwholesome Talk

"What is that word, Mommy?" Brooke asked, pointing to graffiti sprayed on a wall.

Mom had prayed and prepared for this question! "S—- is a word that people write or say when they want to offend someone else. Sometimes people say words like that when they feel small or helpless. They think saying it will make them feel bigger and more powerful."

Stop and Think

"But what does it mean?"

"Remember the hamster your brother had?" Brooke nodded. "Hamsters eat like we do. When they need to get rid of the waste though, it comes out from under their tails. S—- is a slang word for that waste," Mom explained.

Brooke scratched her forehead. Then she said, "So you mean when the hamster goes to the bathroom? Gross! Why would someone want to say that?"

Brooke's mom smiled. "Everything gets rid of waste— fish, birds, beavers, camels, giraffes, even trees!"

Brooke's eyes went wide, and she exclaimed, "Mommy, trees do not go to the bathroom!"

"Tree waste is not like human or animal waste. Tree waste is oxygen. Trees lose oxygen through little holes in their leaves. God planned it this way. Humans and animals need oxygen; we breathe out the carbon dioxide that trees need to live," she answered.

"Okay, but what about the other part—you know."

"Fish are a good example of that," Mom said. "Their liquid waste goes back into the lake and provides chemicals needed by other small organisms and plants. The solid waste that drops down to the soil layer is also used. The same is true for the waste from all animals and people. God worked it all out."

Brooke looked satisfied and began walking again. After awhile she said, "Why in the world would talking about going to the bathroom make someone feel stronger?"

Look and Listen

Four-letter or "dirty" words usually refer to an animal's or person's private functions. These words make normal acts seem dirty or ugly. (Here you might ask your children if they've heard any ugly words and wondered what they mean. Often understanding the true meaning of a word defuses the power and mystique of that word.) Do you think God designed animals, plants, or people with any dirty or nasty parts? Check out what He says in Genesis 1:31.

Actually, these bad words grieve God. Look at Ephesians 4:29–32. Unwholesome talk meant to harm someone else is *malice* (verse 31). Sometimes unwholesome talk is said in anger and rage (verse 31). These words never benefit those who listen (verse 29).

Wholesome and unwholesome talk struggle to share the same mouth. David asked God to put a soldier by his mouth to make sure only good came out:

Set a guard over my mouth, O LORD; keep watch over the door of my lips (Psalm 141:3).

God sighting. Ask God to set a soldier by your mouth to keep those words from coming out. Write the words you don't want to say on a piece of paper. Pray David's prayer now specifically about those words. Watch for God's help to keep you from saying them. If you do not need help with this difficulty, you might pray together for a neighbor or extended family member.

Proceed with Care

✔ Mouths can be used for lots of good things. For example, mix up a pan of bubble soap: ¼ cup dishwashing soap (Joy brand works best), ¼ cup water, 1 teaspoon sugar, and 1 tablespoon glycerin (you can get this at a drugstore). Put a pinhole in the bottom of a Styrofoam cup. Dip the top in the bubble soap and blow great big bubbles!

✔ Here's another bubble idea: Mix 1 tablespoon dish soap, 4 tablespoons water, and 1 tablespoon food coloring in a small jar so that the liquid is close to the jar's lip. Blow bubbles with a straw in the jar. Quickly cover the area with manila or white construction paper. Bubble prints will appear. Let dry. Change the color by adding new food coloring. Blow again and catch the bubbles on the same paper. Notice the combination of shapes and colors!

✔ Sweeten up your mouth with some homemade mints. You'll need the following: 1 pound powdered sugar, 4 teaspoons salt, ⅓ cup corn syrup, 1 unbeaten egg white, ¼ cup shortening, ½ tablespoon peppermint flavoring or extract. Mix all the ingredients and knead thoroughly. Form small balls and flatten. Set on waxed paper to dry.

✔ Have fun with fold-over stories. Each person in the family fills in one blank. Fold over the paper so the next person can't see the previous answer. Here is the story (possible answers appear in parentheses):

(1) **Once a person named** _____ (Mike) (2) **met a person named** _____ (Julie) (3) **at** _____ (the ice-cream store). (4) **The first person said,** _____ ("Did you take a cookie?") (5) **and the other person answered,** _____ ("It's raining"). (6) **So** _____ (they got mad at each other), (7) **and it ended with the words:** _____ ("Go brush your teeth"). God gives us imagination to make up funny stories!

✔ Draw a face puppet on your fist as illustrated. Have one puppet try to out-compliment the other!

GOOD JOB!

WAY TO GO!

RAY TO RO, REORGE!

✔ Finish this free verse:

My tongue searches inside its empty cavern,
Then something enters and brings such delight—
The taste of _____, _____, and _____,
Everything in harmony.
My tongue flips and curls as the words blow out,
Sweet words bringing such delight—
The sound of _____, _____, and _____,
Everything in harmony.

God created animals to praise His glory with their bodies. They each "speak" a language of barks, trills, roars, clicks, and whistles. Sing a praise song to the tune of "Beautiful Savior, King of Creation" using the language of animals! Add barks, roars, and beeps if you feel adventurous!

Go in Peace

Jesus Is the Way to Eternal Life

Stop and Think

The road sign pointed in six different directions. It said: "This way to the Golden City." Tracy threw up her hands in disgust. "Now how am I supposed to find the way to the Golden City?"

"They all go to the city," said a cat sitting in a nearby tree. "You can stand still and get to the Golden City because it is everywhere."

"That's ridiculous! I'm not in a city!" Tracy stamped her foot while the cat flicked his tail.

"How do you know you're not in the city? Maybe this really is the city, and you just don't know it."

The thought puzzled Tracy, but then she remembered something. "This is not the city because in the real city everyone can see the king. And you are not the king!" The cat's eyes glinted wickedly, and in an instant, he vanished.

Tracy stared at the sign. "Which way is the right way?" she muttered. A rabbit bounced into view. "Stop!" Tracy called. "Please tell me the way to the Golden City."

The rabbit turned and said, "It doesn't matter which road you take so long as you're very sincere about your journey."

Tracy stared at the rabbit's twitchy whiskers. Then she said, "That doesn't make sense. I can very sincerely take the

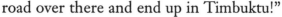

road over there and end up in Timbuktu!"

"It doesn't matter where you end up! The journey is the thing," bristled the rabbit.

Tracy frowned. "It matters to me that I end up in the Golden City to see the king!"

The rabbit sniffed at Tracy disdainfully. "You just don't get it. Humph!" And with a leap, he was gone.

Tracy plopped down in the middle of the road, facing the signs. She noticed two dormice sitting very still, also facing the signs. "Oh, Miss Dormouse," Tracy whispered to the smaller one, "can you tell me the way to the Golden City?"

"You must lose all these desires, child. The true way to happiness is to empty yourself of any wants. Meditate on the great mysteries like our teacher, Budaor," the little creature answered. She glanced over Tracy in a languid way.

"Don't listen to her! She's been sitting there talking mysteries as long as anyone can remember!" The older dormouse snorted in disgust.

"Some mice spend all their time bowing up and down on rugs, facing east and keeping track of who breaks which rules," the younger mouse answered slowly. The older one began to argue but gave up when the first mouse closed her eyes.

"How will I know the way to the Golden City?" Tracy cried in frustration.

Just then a dove spiraled around the trees and came gently down on Tracy's shoulder. "From up above, I can see the Golden City. Keep your eyes on me, I will lead you to the king."

"Why should I follow you?" Tracy asked.

"I've come from the Golden City just now to find you. I know the road. It is narrow and the way is hard, but when you follow me, you will get to the king. None of these others has ever been to the city. I am the way."

Read John 14:6 (a good verse to memorize). How is Jesus like the dove in Tracy's story? The disciple, Philip, was asking Jesus for the way to God the Father. What did Jesus tell him? Read John 14:9–11. Philip had spent a lot of time with Jesus, enough time to realize that Jesus talked and acted just like God the Father had always talked and acted. If Tracy spent a lot of time with the dove, she'd learn whether the dove was truthful or not. As we spend time with Jesus by reading the Bible, listening to others tell of Him, and getting to know Him through prayer, we also learn that Jesus is truthful.

Jesus reminded Philip of all the miracles He'd done. His miracles were done out of love. Jesus did things only God can do—healing people, stilling storms, turning water into wine. Jesus knows the way to heaven because He came from heaven to get us!

Many people have different beliefs about the way to heaven. Some say that meditating and chanting will get you there. Others say that keeping rules and being more good than bad will get you there. Many believe in all sorts of gods, some who are nice and others who are mean. They try to cater to the nice ones for favors and bribe the mean ones to avoid bad luck. Some people even believe that all ways lead to heaven so long as you are sincerely trying to get there. Jesus said, "No one comes to the Father except through Me." We know that Jesus is the only way to heaven.

God sighting. Look for "one way" street signs this week. Say a little prayer thanking Jesus for showing you the way to Him.

✔ Take a penny hike with your family. Walk one block, then toss the penny—heads means go right, tails means go left. Have the children mark the trail so that you can find your way back. Try tree walks (look for different leaves or bark), full-moon walks (trace around some of the shadows you see), or insect walks (take a magnifying glass!).

✔ Plan a mystery journey in your house. Work backwards from your "Golden City" where Dad might be waiting with a paper crown on his head. For example, if the city is in the guest room closet, the clue found in the bathtub could read: "You are nearly there. The final destination is somewhere that can be dark or light." The clue before this one directs searchers to the bathroom and reads: "You are traveling on the correct path! Seek a spot where it sometimes rains, sometimes floods, and sometimes is as dry as a desert."

✔ As Abraham traveled, he often stopped to pray after he had experienced God in a special way. In that spot, he set up stones as a spiritual marker along his journey. Jacob, his grandson, set one up where he saw the ladder to heaven. Joshua placed 12 stones together to mark where the Israelites crossed into the Promised Land. Undoubtedly there have been times when you felt particularly close to God or you learned something significant in your relationship with God. Let each person in your family gather several stones and talk about these spiritual markers. Then pile the stones somewhere where they are visible to remind you that God is with you always on your journey.

✔ Glue cereal pieces in an arrow outline. Turn the arrow so that it points up. Title it "Jesus is the Way." Hang your arrow on the front door and give other arrows to friends or to the church secretary to hang on the church's front door.

This is where we are going, "to Mount Zion, to the heavenly Jerusalem, the city of the living God ... to thousands upon thousands of angels in joyful assembly, to the church of the firstborn, whose names are written in heaven" (Hebrews 12:22–23). Your name is written already in heaven! Jesus is already your Way! Tell God what this means to you!

Go in Peace

God Creates Each Person with Unique Talents

"Everybody's better than me. I can't do anything," cried Chris. He put his face down on the desk. Miss Page rubbed his back and moved his smudged essay to one side.

Stop and Think

"Nothing's going right," she reflected.

"No, I can't do schoolwork as well as Brad. I can't make baskets like Chad. I can't draw like Brandon. I'm just stupid." Chris lifted his head. "You said God doesn't make junk, but you're wrong. I'm junk!"

"Junk, Chris?" Miss Page said softly. "Junk gets thrown away. You are too precious to throw away." Miss Page continued, "Who did the class vote wagon master when we crossed the United States on the Oregon Trail? Who makes everyone laugh? Who said kind words to Jenna when she fell on the soccer field?"

"Well, but I'm not good at things that are important," Chris argued.

"What's important, Chris?"

"Being smart and good at sports or drawing or writing," he answered.

"Can I tell you something?" Miss Page asked. Chris nodded. "Once there were animals who decided that they all should be good at everything—running, climbing, swimming, and flying. The duck did well with swimming, but climbing got him a D. The rabbit got an A in running but an F in flying. The fish did superior work in swimming but mangled her fins running. The frog did amazingly well in everything! The others had just decided that being a frog was the best until a badger insisted burrowing must be included. Then even the frog felt discouraged. Life seemed gray for all of them as they compared themselves to each other. Soon they were all miserable."

What was Miss Page trying to tell Chris?

Look and Listen

Teacher-training classes talk about "multiple intelligences": verbal, logical, visual, body, rhythmic, interpersonal, and intrapersonal. For years people believed there were only three talents: intellectual, athletic, or artistic. Think of the talents God gives us:

1. **Knees**—Humility leads people to get eye to eye with others, to pray for those in trouble, and to help with chores, such as scrubbing, dusting, and putting gas in the family car. Gardeners, homemakers, prayer partners, and telephone repair people use knee gifts.
2. **Feet**—Peacefulness helps people walk away from those who provoke them or leave when others gossip. God also gives the gift of quickness for people to delight in dancing, playing sports, or simply running for the joy of it. Professional and Olympic athletes, troubleshooters, and ambassadors use feet skills.
3. **Hands**—Dexterity is a marvelous gift from God. With this ability people build churches, sew doll clothes, paint, and play instruments. Doctors, nurses, mechanics, chauf-

feurs, parts makers, architects, and skilled craftspeople use these hand talents. Generosity or open-handedness is a branch of this gift too.

4. **Mouths**—Kindness, so necessary in the world, often goes unnoticed. Kind people use words that build others up. God gives kind people an extra big place in their hearts for caring. This gift comes with good listening skills and patience. Social workers, singers, pastors, and comedians use this gift to bring love to others.

5. **Brains**—People with wisdom know how to avoid mistakes and speak the truth about how God's creation works. These individuals help us by instruction and example. Teachers, engineers, managers, researchers, and organizers are people who help us make the most out of our skills.

6. **Elbows**—Flexibility reminds everyone not to get stuck to one way of doing things. People with this gift often see unique and creative ways to do things. Cartoonists, advertisers, designers, and people who tinker often use their flexibility to help us open our eyes to new possibilities.

7. **Eyes**—Clarity means to see things clearly. People with this gift make sense out of the most confusing situations. Counselors, personnel people, and consultants can sort out the facts that matter most. Another eye gift is insight. People with this gift can look at a situation and know just where to help.

Discuss with your family the talents you see in one another. You might even refer to a generational talent like "You have your grandpa's generosity" or "Those long piano fingers are like Aunt Danielle's."

God sighting. Write each of the above talents on a card. Every day, look for a different talent in the people around you. Talk about what you've seen at supper or bedtime. Increase your awareness of the abundance of talents God gives His people. Remember, no one but Jesus has every talent. God gave His perfect, talented Son for our sins!

Proceed with Care

- ✔ Use your musical talents! Hang up metal objects like cookie racks, pots, a potato masher, garage tools, and old parts. Then "play" your masterpiece melody using a soup ladle! Or arrange glasses or glass jars in a line and fill them with graduated levels of water. Clink a spoon against each glass. Hear the different tones! Try to play a tune, such as "Row, Row, Row Your Boat" or "Happy Birthday."
- ✔ Try out those flexible fingers. Attach a string to the center of an upside-down paper cup. Connect the other end of the string to a broomstick handle. Who can get the cup on the broomstick the most times?
- ✔ How good are your eyes? Set out 10 objects in front of your family for 30 seconds. Tell family members to look the other way, then remove one of the objects, or reverse two objects for older children. Ask them to tell you what has changed.
- ✔ Host a Readers Gala. Everyone reads or recites a favorite poem, excerpt from a book, Bible verse, or picture book. Make bookworm invitations together and decide on your menu. A high tea with various teas, scones, petit fours, tarts, and fruits is fun!
- ✔ Exercise your creativity. Start to draw an object on a sheet of paper. Then pass it to another person to finish it. How different were your ideas?

✔ Architect alert: Build a city or a castle using cooked cold peas and toothpicks. The peas serve as the stabilizing joints. Let it dry. Or if you live by a beach, do evening sand creations. In China, there is a Moon Festival celebration on the beach that delights everyone. People surround sand castles with all the old candles collected during the year. This is a good time to enjoy candlelight in the night air and give thanks to God for the beautiful sandy beaches He created.

Paul mentions many talents in 1 Corinthians 13, but he says love is the most significant gift of all. Pray 1 Corinthians 13:4–6, substituting "Jesus" for "love"

Jesus is patient, Jesus is kind. Jesus does not envy, Jesus does not boast, Jesus is not proud. Jesus is not rude, Jesus is not self-seeking, Jesus is not easily angered, Jesus keeps no record of wrongs. Jesus does not delight in evil but rejoices with the truth.

Ask God to help you be more like Jesus.

Go in Peace

The Holy Spirit Works inside Us

Brad listened intently. His Sunday school teacher had asked everyone to bring a friend to the Friendship Festival in two weeks. The way she asked surprised Brad. She said, "I know it's embarrassing to ask someone. Maybe when you were 6 or 7, it was easier, but now that you're 10, what if they laugh at you? But you don't have to just go up to someone and start talking."

Stop and Think

Brad leaned forward. Mike was a friend whom Brad often played with at recess, but Mike sometimes teased Brad. It didn't seem to bother Mike when Brad walked off to sit by himself under a tree. Brad knew that if Mike could get closer to Jesus, things would be better. No way could I just walk up and say, "Hey, Mike, how about coming to church with me Sunday," thought Brad.

His teacher continued, "The very first thing you do is start praying. You ask God to help you use your gift of the Holy Spirit. You see, the Holy Spirit first came to live in your heart when you were a new believer. But we all keep big parts of our hearts to ourselves." She drew a big heart on the board. In the center she drew a small circle and put a cross in it. "Everything that's not in this circle is not centered on Jesus. When we ask for help from the Spirit, then the Spirit moves into more territory." She widened the circle on the board.

"Open your Bibles to Acts 4:24–31." The children read the verses together. "Peter and John had just been released from jail after they testified about Jesus to the same court that had condemned Him only two months before. The Christians thanked God and then prayed for the boldness to speak about Jesus even more. Look what happened!"

Brad had never heard this part before. He leaned forward, listening intently.

"You see, the Holy Spirit began working inside these early Christians. If you remember, after 3,000 were baptized, they began caring about one another. The Spirit did that first. Then the Spirit prompted them to speak out without worrying about being ridiculed or mistreated."

Brad pictured himself talking with Mike about God very calmly, just like talking about baseball statistics. Facts are facts—and Jesus is a fact! Brad told himself.

"One more thing," the teacher said. "Ask God to prepare

the heart of the person you'll talk to. Ask Jesus to help point that person's thoughts toward God. Then let God be the One to put that friend in your path."

Brad had been leaning forward so long he almost fell over. "If the Holy Spirit makes me unafraid, gets Mike ready, and shows me the timing, then this whole thing would be pretty amazing." Brad didn't realize he'd spoken aloud.

Brad's teacher smiled. "What do you mean 'if'? Don't you mean 'when'?"

Look and Listen

Brad is a real person. At age 11, Brad became part of his church's evangelism team. He helped many people talk about God. The Holy Spirit worked in Brad to give him that boldness.

The Bible tells us of a man who became bold. Peter, the disciple, never looked before he leaped. One time he threw his fishing net over when Jesus told him to do it and caught so many fish that the boat nearly sank. Afterwards he realized Jesus was not ordinary, that Jesus was who He said He was—the Son of God. So Peter got confused and said, "Depart from me for I am a sinful man." That's not what you want to say to Jesus is it?

Another time Peter saw Jesus walking on the water and decided to follow Him. Peter leapt overboard. He sank like a stone!

Once Peter dashed over to the courtyard of the high priest so he could see Jesus, who'd been dragged off to court. Peter braved the temple guards until some people said he might be Jesus' friend. Peter's courage vanished, and he denied he even knew Jesus!

But after Pentecost, when Peter received the Holy Spirit, he was a different man. Not only did he speak to the citizens who'd earlier yelled, "Crucify Him," but he spoke boldly to the court that had plotted Jesus' death all along! Peter changed from a wimp to a warrior. Look at the story in Acts 4:1–21.

How did Peter change? The same way you are changing. Your heart is the Spirit's workplace. Think of it like a house. You might have prayed for God to help you stop putting off your homework, gossiping, or being jealous. So the Holy Spirit begins knocking out a window in your heart house. That problem clears up, but guess what—the Spirit is on a roll! He not only knocks out a wrong window, He knocks down the whole wall! He's making your house bigger. After that, maybe He'll start working on your prayer closet or maybe on that spooky basement room where your fears hide. Maybe the Spirit will put some forgiveness vents in your heart's attic to let those old, smoldering grudges out. Where do you think the Spirit is working in you?

God sighting. Do you know any Christian who is noticeably changing? People don't become more loving, joyful, peaceful, patient, kind, good, faithful, gentle, or self-controlled without help from the Holy Spirit! When you see this, you've seen God at work.

Proceed with Care

- ✔ Use both sides of nine paper plates to show the faces of a person the Holy Spirit has changed from selfish to loving, pessimistic to joyful, anxious to peaceful, and the other six fruit of the Spirit listed in Galatians 5:22–23. Label and pin these faces to a curtain for this week. Which face do you want right now?

- ✔ Decide on a building project—maybe a house out of blocks or a Lego castle or an Erector set high-rise. The Holy Spirit is always working to build us up to be like Jesus, and He knocks down any selfish attitudes in us.

- Make up a batch of heart-shaped sugar cookies. Draw a circle in the center of each and drop a bit of red jam inside. Talk about the Spirit in our hearts.

- Play the Goodness Game. Give each person four M&M's candies, pecans, or pretzel sticks. Take turns rolling a die and doing what the number says: (1) give one piece to the player on your left; (2) give one piece to the player on your right; (3) sing a short song and eat one of your pieces; (4) take one person's piece and give it to someone else; (5) choose someone who can eat one of his or her pieces; (6) give one of your pieces to someone else to eat when he or she has given you a high five.

- We build each other up when we affirm the fruit of the Spirit in each other as we see them. Here is a list of affirmations. See which you might like to use more often.

  - [ ] Thank you for waiting patiently.
  - [ ] I think you'll make a good parent someday because you're so gentle.
  - [ ] My day is better when I see your face.
  - [ ] Putting that together took so much persistence—wow!
  - [ ] Thank you for being generous.
  - [ ] That took a lot of courage.
  - [ ] You know, you spoke the truth in love that time.
  - [ ] You handled that very wisely.
  - [ ] I can trust you with more responsibility now.
  - [ ] You really stayed calm.
  - [ ] That showed a lot of self-control.
  - [ ] You have a lot of teacher qualities.
  - [ ] You plan ahead, and things don't pile up on you.

- [ ] You make groups more lively and fun.
- [ ] I'm amazed at what you do with your hands.
- [ ] You're a real helper.

Go in Peace

Stand in a circle and give each person a tool, such as a hammer, screwdriver, rake, scissors, or wire cutter. The Spirit is always at work in us. What does each of your tools suggest to you about what the Spirit is doing? After discussion, praise God for the work the Holy Spirit does in each of you.

God Makes the Church Jesus' Hands and Feet

Stop and Think

Inside your wall are wires running to different parts of your house. All those wires eventually connect outside to the main cables that run all over the city. Those huge cables run from all over the city to the power plant where electricity is produced. So when you decide you want light or you want the radio on, you switch on the light bulb or turn on the radio and make a connection with electricity.

Your body doesn't work that way! Your body is "wired" with nerves that run all over the place inside, and all those nerves connect to your spinal cord and brain. But when someone outside connects your hand to a pencil, it doesn't start writing. Or when your head connects to a pillow, you don't automatically close your eyes. You do have electric impulses that make your muscles do things. But outside forces don't "turn you on." Your brain switches you to "on."

Imagine what life would be like if your brain weren't in control. Suppose there were lots of power supervisors around. If one of them put shoes on your feet, you'd walk until another one took them off. If one put a fork in your hand, you'd eat everything on your plate and keep putting the fork in your mouth until someone took it out of your hand. If one turned your head to watch a tennis game, your head would keep turning until someone stopped it. After awhile, you'd probably wonder why you had a brain at all!

God didn't make our bodies that way. Instead, God made each person the power supervisor of himself or herself. Your brain sends power down your nerve endings in your eyelids, fingers, knees, and toes. Your brain has an automatic pilot system built in by God to run the routines of breathing, pumping blood, and digestion so the power supervisor can focus on its options.

God could have made the church like a house. If He did, then people would come there, plug into the Spirit's power, and go off about their daily tasks. Most false religions are set up this way. The religion is private. The congregation really isn't necessary.

Instead God made His church like a body. Each of us is not separate. We do not plug into energy that's "wired in." Instead, the body of Christ is run by the Head of the church, the brain—Jesus. Jesus lets the members of His body—that's you and me—know what He wants to do. If He wants to soothe a hurting spot in His body, He sends His mercy people to the hurting person. If He wants to reach out and bring back a lost person, He sends a message to His evangelism members and energizes them. If He wants to feed His body, He gets materials to His volunteer teachers, and they get to work.

Every person in Christ's body has a function just like every fingernail and eyelash on your body has a purpose. What do you think is your function in your church?

Look and Listen

Read 1 Corinthians 12:4–27. What are some of the "body parts" the Spirit gives your church? (See verses 8–10.) If you received the gift of knowledge, would you have that just so you could get good grades in school, go to a good college, and get a high-paying job? (See verse 7.) How might a person whose function is knowledge help everyone else in the body?

Suppose you're just a little pinkie finger in the church. Are you unimportant to the body? (See verse 25.) What if you're an eye in the church. Are you more important? (See verses 17–19.)

What if every person in your church was just alike, full of faith, wisdom, trust, knowledge, compassion, *and* love for others? Wouldn't that be the best church? It doesn't work that way here on earth. God knows we are not perfect people. So first of all, He sets up the church to wait for directions from the Head of the church, Jesus. He puts some members in it to understand what Jesus is telling the church to do. He puts in others to serve, listen, heal, organize, and envision. All the people in His church have something important to do, just like all the parts of our human bodies. All the people in Christ's church need each other too. God wants us to depend on the brain first and then on each other.

When Jesus was on earth, He had a human body. Now Jesus calls *us* His body. Churches filled with His energizing Spirit are sent to do tasks by Him. We really are His hands, feet, eyes, ears, and mouth on this earth. Wow! What a privilege!

God sighting. Who in your church can you see Jesus directing to administer, evangelize, teach, preach, encourage, pray, help, give generously, or share wisdom? (These are some of the gifts of the Spirit mentioned in the Bible.)

Proceed with Care

✔ If there's a place in your house with no windows, cram your family in there! Give them paper and pencils to draw pictures of one another. Come out and see your pictures. How are eyes important for a task? Then on another piece of paper, try to draw again, using a pencil stuck between your toes. Use your other foot to hold the paper down. How are hands important for a task? Once more, on another piece of paper, try to draw your family while you run in place, sing "Jingle Bells," and nod your head, all at the same time. How is having some body parts at rest while others are working important for a task? When every person in the church body isn't using his or her particular gifts for Jesus, what happens with the tasks?

How do we keep our bodies in shape? Give each person a paper plate. Ask, "What would be good for your body to have on a plate for the main meal?" Let each draw answers. (A good answer is fruit, vegetables, carbohydrates, and proteins.) Exercise by doing 10 minutes of aerobics, calisthenics, or an active game together. Rent an exercise videotape for fun. Talk about sleep habits while you're resting from the exercises. If you all lie down on the living room floor and one of you says, "Relax your chest … Breathe in … and out … in … and out … Now stiffen your arms … Now relax your arms … Now stiffen your hands … Now relax your hands … " and so on with muscles, you will find yourself near sleep! Conclude with cleanliness by washing hands together in the sink—all the right hands at once, then all the left hands. We're responsible for taking care of our bodies just as we are responsible for caring for our church members too.

✔ Ponder this: Wouldn't it be easier for God to do all the tasks of a church by Himself? He's a great healer, very organized, knows everything, and can do miracles. So why does He need us to help?

- ✔ Everyone has tasks in a family. Every person in a family is needed—even a baby. A baby can teach the rest of the family about patience, sacrifice, and gentleness. Have each person say one to three things that he or she does to help the family manage. (Remember gifts of humor, peacemaking, praying, etc., are needed too.)

- ✔ Make people out of play dough. Make your own play dough by mixing 2 cups flour, ½ cup salt, 2 tablespoons alum (from the drugstore), and 1 tablespoon oil. Pour this into 1½ cups boiling water. Stir briefly. Cool and knead. Store in an airtight zipper bag.

- ✔ Have a family member lie on a sheet of newspaper. (Tape several pieces together if you need to.) Trace around the person and cut out the shape. Then cut apart the hands, feet, arms, legs, and head. Pass out the parts, including the trunk. How is each part important? What do you like about each part? (Good for tickling, good for leaning on, good for hugging, etc.)

Go in Peace

If your thumb could talk, what kind things would it say to the rest of your body? What kind words could you say to your church members? Thank God for making us part of His body, the church.

God Placed Us in His Unique Kingdom

"What's that?" Max asked his mom.

Mrs. Ferranti fingered the pendant on her necklace. "It's a mustard seed, Max. Here, look." She leaned down and let Max hold the small globe near his good eye. A tiny seed balanced in the center of clear plastic. "Micah brought it back from England when his youth group from church toured there."

Stop and Think

"A seed is a funny thing to wear in a necklace," Max commented as he let the pendant drop.

"If we planted one of these, it would grow into a plant as tall as a man on a horse! There is a story about a pastor named George Mueller who believed that Jesus can make big things out of small things like mustard seeds."

Max sat on a stool at the kitchen counter. He liked stories and knew his mother was going to tell one. Just then Micah came through the kitchen looking for a snack. "Oh, Micah, I was just going to tell Max about George Mueller."

"I heard about Pastor Mueller when I was in Bristol," Micah said. "He lived there over a hundred years ago."

"What did he do?" Max asked. Mrs. Ferranti nodded to Micah to tell the story.

So Micah began, "Pastor Mueller felt that people didn't believe God really would do anything miraculous anymore. They felt poor and powerless. So Pastor Mueller asked God to give him some way to show people that He could do amazing things.

"Very soon he noticed the large number of street kids whose parents had died. These children grew up without a place to call home. So Pastor Mueller felt God wanted him to do something about that. He began to pray for the money and supplies he needed. Two days later he got 20 cents! But he continued to pray, not telling anyone how much he needed.

"He was soon able to rent a large house and fill it with donated furniture and blankets. In a short time, this house was overflowing, so he prayed for another house. In only months, a third house was opened! Soon he had room and board for 96 children!

"Every morning Pastor Mueller and his helpers prayed for what they needed. God never sent huge amounts, but supplies and money came regularly. For example, one day the pantry shelves were bare. The children sat at the table, and Pastor Mueller prayed, "Father, we thank You for the food You're going to give us." Just then a baker knocked and said, "I felt the Lord wanted me to make this bread for you." A few minutes later a milkman knocked. "My wagon broke down in front of your house, and I need to get rid of all the milk before I can get the wagon fixed. Will you take it?"

"By the end of Pastor Mueller's life, he'd built four orphanages and cared for more than 10,000 children. He had received more than $8,000,000 in answer to his prayers and never asked anyone except God for help." Micah leaned over to grab an apple from the bowl. "And it all started with 20 cents."

Mrs. Ferranti looked at Max. "You might think the tithe of your allowance isn't much, Max, but God can do a lot with it. You might think you don't do much during the church service, but the Bible says the praise of children silences God's enemies (Psalm 8:2). God can take anything you say or do out of love for Him and make it grow."

Max pointed to the seedlings growing on the windowsill. "God is an expert at growing things." Micah and his mom laughed.

Read Jesus' parable in Matthew 13:31–32. Jesus told stories to help us understand how His kingdom works. Because His thinking is so much wiser than ours, He spent a lot of time on earth teaching us about heaven.

Most people think you need to have lots of money or a powerful position to make big changes happen. In the kingdom of heaven, life isn't like that. Instead God says He "hears the prayers of the righteous" (Proverbs 15:29). That means one person talking to God and obeying—like George Mueller—and making huge changes.

Some people believe the superstars, political figures, or top athletes are important. In the kingdom of heaven, Jesus says, "whoever wants to be first must be your slave" (Matthew 20:27). Who's important? Servants like Jesus. God's blessings are unlimited. Jesus says, "Seek first His kingdom and His righteousness, and all these things will be given to you as well" (Matthew 6:33). He reminds us that just as He keeps all the plants and animals, so He can supply us too.

Reading the Bible will teach us even more about our King and His kingdom.

God sighting. How does God want us to treat our enemies? (He wants us to love them and pray for them.) Pray that God will work in your spirit when you are with a person who irritates you. Then watch to see what happens in your thoughts and actions. Don't forget to thank God for His help when you notice the change!

✔ Buy large lima bean seeds. Write the following references on several sets of five seeds: Mark 9:23; Romans 8:38–39; Philippians 3:8; Hebrews 10:19–22; Colossians 3:3; and Isaiah 43:1–2. Put the five seeds into 10 homemade envelopes folded like seed packets. Write "Seeds of Faith" on the front of the packets. Decorate the packets with leaves. On the back write "Directions: Remove a seed and read the passage from the Bible. To plant the words in your heart, write the entire passage on a card and tape the seed to the card. Put it in a place where you'll see it often. When the words take root in your spirit, plant the next seed." Give your packets to your friends and to your pastor to use on hospital visits.

✔ Jesus said the kingdom of heaven grows like yeast into bread dough. Make bread together and let the children add the yeast. If you play with the dough as if it were clay for fun, that will count as kneading! Measure the dough with a piece of string. After the dough has risen, try to stretch the string around it while it is in the bowl. (Deduct a little for the bowl.) Our church grows this way too—one Christian touches the next.

✔ Make a graph-paper design. Start by coloring the center square. Work out from there coloring squares connected to the center square using one, two, or three colors in a pattern. Continue working outward from the second set of squares to the third and so on. When done, remember that your large, complex design all started with one figure, just like the Christian church started with one person, Jesus.

✔ Begin a piggy bank for a charity or person at your church. Pray for guidance from Jesus about which charity or person to give to. Don't tell anyone about the bank. Just set it on the counter. Every time unexpected money comes to the family, put the money in the bank and thank God together. Have fun watching the cash grow. Remember—pray for the charity or person and give thanks to God every time money arrives.

If you want to astonish the family and watch money pile up, charge *everyone* 10 cents per half hour of TV viewing—even yourself!

✔ How far can you go with this poem?

> One young child said, "Jesus is true."
> His friend believed and that made two.
> Two friends said, "Of sin we're free."
> Another joined and that made three.
> Three friends prayed, "Your love outpour."
> A schoolmate came and that made four ...

What impresses you the most about God or His kingdom? After discussing this, turn the words into your prayer.

Go in Peace

God Delights Us with the Desires of Our Hearts

Stacy helped the department store Santa lift children on and off his lap. She'd already worked the first 10 days of December, and though her arms were getting stronger, her heart was sore. "The children all seem the same," she thought as she lifted down a hefty youngster. "Santa talks a little to

Stop and Think

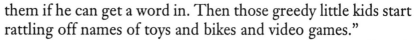

them if he can get a word in. Then those greedy little kids start rattling off names of toys and bikes and video games."

Stacy looked at the child with a white coat now on Santa's lap. She pictured Santa asking her if the video game he gave her last year made her happy. I wonder if last year's presents even got used this past week, Stacy thought.

Some of the children in line sure didn't seem happy. One was pulling on her mother's skirt, demanding gum. Another teased his little sister in the stroller. One was even trying to rip the Santa sign.

Stacy looked at Santa. The little girl on his lap seemed to be in earnest conversation. Santa talked on and off too. Stacy leaned a little closer to listen. "Well, Joyce," Santa said, "you've asked for something that I can't really manage. But I know Someone who can." He touched the side of his nose, and his eyes twinkled.

"Who?" asked little Joyce.

"All the really important presents come from God. You want a friend. That's one of those really important presents. You talk to Him about that, and I will too."

Joyce nodded and began to scoot down. "Is there anything else you'd like to ask for, for Christmas?" Santa asked.

"Nope. A friend would really make me happy." She got her feet to the floor and headed over to her dad, waiting by the exit sign. Santa and Stacy gazed after her.

"There goes a wise little lady," Santa said.

Stacy smiled and reached for a baby. Babies didn't talk. They just got a picture taken.

I wonder what this mother will ask Santa for, for her baby. Would it be some toy, or would it be a deep feeling of being loved? pondered Stacy. Then she remembered what Santa had said to the girl in the white cap—all the really important presents come from God.

Often we don't know the desires of our hearts, the lasting joys, until after God has given them to us. Fortunately, God is the Giver of the important things, and He knows exactly what our hearts desire.

Look for the "important presents" listed in Psalm 103.

- ✔ being so connected with God that my inner being praises Him spontaneously
- ✔ being forgiven and healed of disease in my body and in my spirit
- ✔ being saved from eternal death
- ✔ knowing that God values me and gives me love and compassion
- ✔ knowing God is working righteousness and justice in me
- ✔ having my sins removed so I can go on without them
- ✔ knowing God is loving to my children's children
- ✔ being a servant doing God's will so that my life and work make a difference

Which of these important presents from God was a desire of your heart that God already satisfied? Which is a desire of your heart that you're asking God to give you?

All the really important presents come from God. He knows the most important and the simpler desires of our hearts. We desire the gift of writing, gardening, fishing, talking on the phone, organizing events, and hosts of other delights. God made us; He knows what yearnings are in each of us.

God sighting. Has God used you to fulfill the desire of someone else's heart? (For instance, by loving that person deeply and letting that person know how much respect you

have for him or her; by sharing work that helps the person change something for the better.)

Proceed with Care

✔ All of us have deeply felt the need to be loved and to give love to those closest to us. If strangers came into your house and looked around, would they be able to tell your family loves one another? Pretend you are strangers. Go to your front door and let yourselves in. Walk from room to room with your "family love" Geiger counter. What things set it off? A table covered with snapshots of the family? The hallway hosting your children's art efforts? The refrigerator door where honors are posted? A photo album set out? Displays of family Baptism certificates or banners? See what you find and what you might want to add.

✔ Ponder this: What is your favorite answered prayer?

✔ God made us with a particular job to do during our lifetime. We are not simply consumers. We get satisfaction from a day of hard work. Do a task as a family: Stuff envelopes for the church or a particular charity, rake and mulch an older neighbor's hedge, draw pictures or write stories and mail them to the children's ward of the local hospital, wash every window inside and out at your child's schoolroom.

✔ Fulfill one of the lighter desires of your hearts by asking each family member to choose something for an upcoming family time. Ideas include visiting a fancy car dealership, pet store, or music shop. Go for a lesson in line dancing, horseback riding, or cooking. Rent bikes in a nearby town. Swim in a hotel pool. Set a skating or bowling date. Make one rule: no complaining! Work hard to let the chooser have a great time.

All of us want to be accepted and esteemed by others who are important to us. Have each family member personalize a balloon person. Photocopy and cut out feet for each family member. Glue the pattern to poster board or cardboard. Blow up a balloon and stick the knot through the hole between the feet. Use markers to add features to the balloons. Have your balloon people say what they'd most like to hear from each other. (Parents: Keep track of the words from your children!)

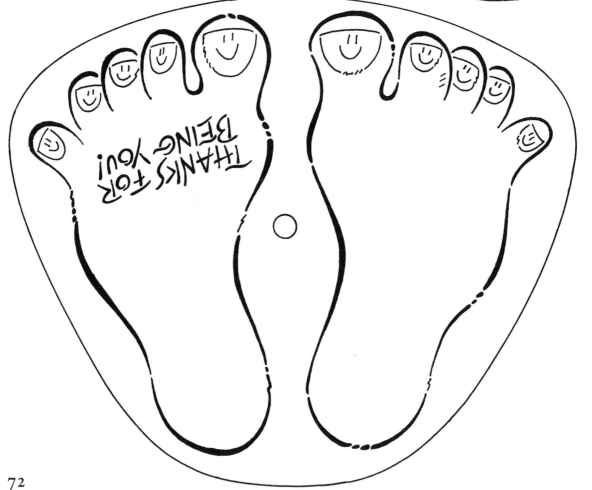

THANKS FOR BEING YOU!

✔ Challenge family members to write "recipes" for each person. For example, the recipe for Dad might be as follows: 2 cups persistence, 3 tablespoons jogging energy, 2 tablespoons laughter, dash of music, handful of questions, and a pinch of mischief.

Bless each other with the words of Psalm 20:

> May the LORD answer you when you
> are in distress;
> may the name of the God of Jacob
> protect you.
> May He send you help from the
> sanctuary
> and grant you support from Zion. …
>
> May He give you the desire of your
> heart
> and make all your plans succeed.
> We will shout for joy when you are
> victorious
> and will lift up our banners in the
> name of our God.
> May the LORD grant all your requests. …
>
> Some trust in chariots and some in
> horses,
> but we trust in the name of the
> LORD our God.

Go in Peace

73

God Hears Us When We Pray

Stop and Think

The stately stone mansion stood at the top of a hill; it was the home of the Lord of the land. The path to the door was narrow but well-worn as various people from near and far sought the wisdom and compassion of the Lord.

Young and old, they came at odd times. In the early morning Reid stopped in with his two sisters, Lauren and Michelle. He was worried about a math test that day at school and needed reassurance that he'd studied well enough.

Shortly after he left, Maggie slipped in with a note asking the Lord to help her parents. They seemed upset about her older brother, and Maggie was sure the Lord could do something.

Midmorning a couple stopped in carrying a heavy box. Apparently they had done some things they were ashamed of, and they wanted to admit it. They stayed inside quite awhile. When they walked out hand in hand, the box was left behind.

At noon old Dr. Larson knocked on the door with flowers in one hand and a cup of tea in the other. At 85, she was still able to climb the hill but liked to visit a bit before walking back. The flowers were from her granddaughter's wedding.

A bit later a mother pushed her toddler up in a stroller. She asked the Lord for a blessing for Brittany. He took the little tike in his arms and cooed at her. Then he blessed her.

At about half past three Valerie sat on the doorstep, head in her hands. Somehow the Lord knew she needed comfort, and he opened the door and sat next to her. "We have to move," she explained. "I don't want to go and leave all my friends." She leaned against him as the Lord talked gently with her. She left with several pictures of her friends that the Lord pulled from his memory book.

All the rest of the afternoon and evening, various people came—asking for advice, permission, and help. They shared their sorrow and gave thanks for the things the Lord had done. The Lord never tired. One only had to knock, and he would open the great oak door.

The last child that evening knocked at about eight o'clock, already in his pajamas. The Lord looked at this little fellow with delight. Mark came every night at 8:00. He leaned down as the boy wrapped his arms around the Lord's neck. The Lord lifted Mark up into his arms. Once there, Mark whispered, "I've made up a song for you."

"What is it?" the Lord asked in wonder.

The song was off-key, and the words very simple. "Oh, I love you. Yes, I love you. You're just my best, best friend, and I love you."

The Lord was deeply touched, and his face glowed as he gave the little fellow one more hug before he scooted home to bed. He waved one last time as Mark turned before passing out of sight. Then the Lord smiled to himself and stretched out his hands wide. "I love you, all my people!" he called. And some who heard the words on the evening wind called back, "And I love you too, my Lord."

Look and Listen

Have you ever wished you could talk to Michael Jordan, the president of the United States, or someone else like that? Is it likely that you could ever get to talk to that person?

God is the most important person in the whole universe. Will you ever get to talk to Him? What does Matthew 7:7–8 say?

God always has time to listen to us. You'll never get a busy signal or an answering machine! He's ready to help any time we ask. We don't have to wait until Sunday. He's available no matter where we are! We can pray under water or in outer space! We can talk to Him about anything—even about not liking pizza when everyone else does!

Name some times of the day when you have talked to God. Name some places where you've talked to God. Name some things you've talked to God about.

Like any person you know, God likes to converse with people He loves. Conversing is something like playing ball. First one person throws the ball, and the other catches it. Then the other throws the ball back to the first person. The ball keeps going back and forth. Prayer is like that too. We throw a concern, a question, or some words of thanks to God. Then He tosses a concern, a question, or some other words back. In prayer we talk and we listen. Imagine what kind of game it would be if you just threw the ball to the other person and never waited for it to come back! Some people pray like that. They toss words to God but don't wait for God to talk back.

How can an invisible God talk? (God talks to us through the Bible, through other thoughts the Holy Spirit brings to mind, and through various circumstances and people.) The reason many people don't hear God is that they've never expected to get a reply. Keeping a prayer list of what we've laid out to God and reviewing it regularly trains us to be ready to catch the ball God tosses back at us.

God sighting. What do you want to hear from God? Write it down and then talk to God about it. Sit quietly at least a minute to get in the habit of listening. Put the card on your pillow, and when you get into bed, think about what you asked God. Did He answer? If so, thank Him. If not yet, put the card on your bedside table so you remember to return it to your pillow in the morning. Keep this up until you hear your answer.

✔ Place your hand on a piece of folded construction paper as illustrated. Trace around your hand and then cut out the hand shape. When you unfold it, spread it apart so that it stands. Write a favorite prayer there or use this one:

> Lord, make me an instrument of Thy peace;
> Where there is hatred, let me sow love;
> Where there is injury, pardon;
> Where there is doubt, faith;
> Where there is despair, hope;
> Where there is darkness, light;
> Where there is sadness, joy.

> *St. Francis of Assisi*

✔ Mail the praying hands to your cousins or other relatives.

✔ David wrote many songs for God in the book of Psalms. Other people wrote songs for God too. Hymn writers and popular Christian artists today write songs of praise. Try writing one using the tune to "Michael Row the Boat Ashore" and these starters:

77

1. Christ, I praise You for this world—Alleluia, for Your _____—Alleluia.
2. Christ, I thank You _____—Alleluia.
3. Christ, forgive me for_____—Alleluia.
4. Christ, I ask _____—Alleluia.

✔ Make a prayer telephone with pictures instead of numbers: health, clothes, shelter, friends, family, useful work, the Bible, our government, and creation. If you dialed your own number, what prayer suggestions would you get? What if you dialed Grandma's number? Use people's phone numbers on this phone as a way to pray for that person.

✔ Play I Hear You. Send one person out of the room and choose a code word. When the person returns, the others should converse, using the code word as often as possible but subtly. When the player is ready to guess, he says, "I hear you" and states the word.

Go in Peace

Plan a motion prayer using Psalm 150. Shape a church with your arms for verse 1. Alternate the motions in verses 3–5.

Jesus Teaches Us to Pray

Stop and Think

While shooting baskets at recess, Alex noticed Micah made almost every shot. He hadn't noticed it before because Micah seldom joined in with Alex's group. A big puddle under the other hoop brought Micah over today.

After Micah's last swish, Alex held the ball and looked at him.

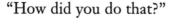

"How did you do that?"

"Come on. Let's play!" answered Micah.

"No. Tell me how come you're hitting so well."

"I started spending time with this friend of mine," Micah answered.

Alex still held the ball. "Who is he?" Some of the other kids gathered round.

"You already know him—Big Sam. He wrote that book on basketball I showed the class. There's lots of good stuff in that book."

The other kids shrugged. Everyone knew Big Sam. He cleaned the school. He'd been a pro player back in his day and loved to tell stories about people back then. The stories were interesting, but who had the time?

"Alex, pass me the ball!" prodded John Mark. Alex looked at Micah and then dribbled away. He took a shot and missed.

Later after school, Alex saw Micah talking to Big Sam. Big Sam moved his elbows, and Micah imitated the move. Sam spotted Alex and waved him over, but Alex had to get home.

The next day during free reading, Alex noticed Micah with Big Sam's old book. As Alex watched, Micah would read a bit, then close his eyes awhile. His lips moved sometimes.

Alex became more interested in that book and dug his copy out of his closet where he'd tossed it years back. He thumbed through the pages, paused, and then sat on his bed. He opened the first page, read a little bit, and then closed his eyes to concentrate on the words. Sometimes his lips moved.

A few days later he shadowed Micah after school so he would be there when Big Sam came by. He joined in their conversation. After a bit Sam said, "I bet Micah here would show you on the court what he's already learned. After that, you and I can talk about your own specific style, and I'll teach you what you need next."

Alex knew Micah's shooting had improved, and Alex wanted to play better too. Admitting that Micah was better came pretty hard. If Micah coached him on the court, then all the guys would know Alex wasn't as good as Micah.

"Let me think about it," Alex answered.

What do you think Alex did? Did he (1) forget the whole thing; (2) swallow his pride and ask Micah for help; or (3) read the book himself and try on his own?

Look and Listen

The disciples had the same Scriptures that Jesus had. They'd memorized parts in synagogue school like He had. They prayed at 9:00, 3:00, and at sunset, but they didn't pray all night as Jesus sometimes did. Still, Jesus seemed to have a whole different connection to God. They had the same choices as Alex. Read Luke 11:1 to see what one of them chose.

Jesus talked to the disciples about praying in Matthew 6:5–15; Luke 6:27–28; Luke 18:1; and Luke 22:40. What did He say? He prayed aloud many times, teaching the disciples how to pray. They heard the familiar prayer in Matthew, prayers of thanks before feeding the 5,000, the parable of the unmerciful servant (Matthew 18:21–35), His prayer in John 17, and even His prayer of forgiveness from the cross.

Have you ever asked Jesus to teach *you* to pray? What might He do if you asked for His help?

God sighting. Pray the prayer, "Jesus, please teach me to pray." Then wait to see what happens.

Proceed with Care

✔ Make a petition-praise journal. Every time you pray together, list your petitions on the left page of a spiral notebook. Make a line to the right page at the same spot. When you're aware of God's answer to a petition, write the praise on the corresponding spot on the right page. Review the journal weekly to see what God is doing.

✔ Hurdle over the obstacles to prayer. Fold paper and cut it in the shape of a hurdle. On each hurdle write one of the following:

☐ Unconfessed and unrepented sin (Psalm 66:18)

☐ Disobedience (Luke 6:46)

☐ Praying without expectation (Philippians 4:6)

☐ Wrong motives (James 4:3)

☐ Ingratitude (Colossians 4:2)

☐ Lack of persistence (Luke 11:5–8)

Ask God to show you if your prayers are hindered by any of these obstacles.

✔ Make a mural using the phrases in the Lord's Prayer.

✔ In John 17, Jesus prayed that we would be unified like Jesus and His Father. He asked His Father to help us be *in God* so that other people in the world would recognize God in action. Read verses 20–26. Does Jesus still pray for us today? (Check Romans 8:34.) Look up *intercede* in the dictionary. Then roleplay interceding so the family clearly understands it. Let Dad intercede in a situation where a child has confessed to Mom about breaking something. Have a child intercede between the parents in a disagreement. Let a parent intercede between a child and another person.

✔ Cut double hearts out of red paper. Then cut a cross shape in the center of both. Sandwich a square of red cellophane between the two hearts and glue the hearts together. Whoever you can see through this heart "window" is someone God loves, someone for whom Jesus intercedes.

✔ Familiarize your family with the books of the Bible. Start with the New Testament. Make bingo grids on paper. Sixteen spaces can hold half the names of the 27 books. Write at least eight different names on each card. Then write the book names on slips of paper for drawing. Play for four in a row or, if you have younger children, three in a row.

✔ Draw a cross on every Band-Aid wrapper in the box as a prayer reminder.

✔ If you looked at Jesus' prayer for the disciples in Matthew 6, notice how He starts His prayer by praising God's name. Then Jesus prays that God's kingdom will come to everyone. He also asks that God's will be done. Jesus is modeling His own words, "Seek first His kingdom and His righteousness and all these things will be added to you as well" (Matthew 6:33). Decide which of the phrases you will emphasize this month. Use washable marker and write various names for God or "Your kingdom come" or "Your will, not mine, be done" on one side of your pillow case.

Write the name of a person you care about on each finger of both hands. Remember helpers like the mail carrier, the grocery store clerk, your school principal, a TV actor, a book writer, as well as loved ones. Then fold your hands and lift each finger in turn as you ask God to bless that person.

Go in Peace

God Helps Us to Forgive

Stop and Think

Andrew pushed the lawn mower down the sidewalk. He'd already done two lawns, and the money felt fat in his back pocket. He hesitated at the end of the next driveway, staring at the house's faded shutters. Mrs. Magill lived there alone now. She hardly ever came outside. Last winter when he shoveled her whole driveway and sidewalk, she only paid him a dollar. "This time I'll tell her how much I charge," he said to himself.

Leaving the lawn mower at the bottom of the porch steps, he mounted the stairs and rang the bell. Mrs. Magill cracked the door. "Hi! I'm Andrew from down the street. I'm mowing lawns for seven dollars, a dollar extra for trimming. Would you like your lawn mowed?" Andrew put on his brightest salesman smile.

Mrs. Magill stood there fishing for something behind the door. Finally she moved one foot out, and Andrew saw her cane. "No, Sonny. I can't afford someone to mow that lawn. I know it needs it, but it'll have to wait until the end of the month." She looked so forlorn that Andrew's heart went out to her.

"That's okay, Mrs. Magill. I'll just cut it to help you out." Mrs. Magill smiled and stepped back inside.

Andrew looked out over the yard from the top of the porch. The upright bricks around the trees and garden areas would be a little tricky. The bush next to the side of the porch blocked his view of the side yard but it was long. He took a deep breath and let it out slowly. Then he moved purposefully down the steps.

By midafternoon, the sun beat down on Andrew. He pulled a rag out of his pocket and wiped his forehead. As he bent down to shut off the mower, he noticed the long edge grass sticking up around the bricks. "I gave her a free mow, I don't need to trim it too," he thought.

Then he looked up at the front window. "Ah," he said, "it won't take me that long, and she'll be happy."

So Andrew grabbed the hand clippers and knelt by the first tree.

Twenty minutes later his back ached, but his heart felt proud. He glanced at the window again, but no one was there. Guess she'll notice it later, he thought.

Andrew bent over to put the clippers back in place, humming to himself. His eye caught some long grass off the side of the porch behind the big bush there. "Oops, missed that." Andrew walked behind the bush. He was just out of sight as old Mrs. Gray came by.

Mrs. Gray marched up to the door, but Andrew kept to his work. He didn't particularly like Mrs. Gray. Mrs. Magill answered her knock. "Hello, Martha. Look at my nice lawn job!" Andrew smiled silently.

"And to think, I got it free too—just by faking out the boy with that old cane of my husband's here. Made him feel sorry for me!"

"You're getting sly in your old age," Martha Gray cackled. Both women laughed.

Andrew's mouth dropped.

Look and Listen

Injustice happens to everyone. It makes people feel violated and outraged. Whether you are betrayed by a friend, falsely accused, treated unfairly, or seriously injured, injustice smarts.

As kids we try to get even so the other person suffers equally. It seems to balance things even though the suffering can't be taken away. God says something startling about this. He says we can't choose to get even—ever! Read Jesus' words in Matthew 5:38–42. What does Jesus say to do when an evil person harms you? Read Matthew 18:15–17. What does Jesus

say to do when a Christian hurts you? Remember that in other places in the Bible, God warns us not to keep close company with wrongdoers, yet He says clearly in Matthew 5:39 to do what? In any case, we are never allowed to get even! Why not? The answer is in Matthew 5:44–45.

If you are a son or daughter of God, then you will act like a member of His family. Christians act the way we see our Father acting. Because He shows us our faults when we sin and treats us with kindness and mercy when we don't deserve it, He expects us to behave as He does toward others.

Fortunately, Christ lives inside us. He overcame the injustice of being treated unfairly and went to the cross willingly to die for sins He did not commit. His strength to forgive injustice is available to us. Because of Jesus, we can let God deal with justice. We can forgive because Jesus has forgiven us.

Proceed with Care

✔ Make the following matching cards: a right cheek and a left cheek, a shirt and a coat, one mile and two miles, a person asking and a person giving, a person borrowing and a person lending, a heart and an enemy, praying hands and hands ready to harm. These are from Matthew 5:39–44. Then play the game Concentration by placing all the cards face down on a table. Players take turns flipping over two cards at a time to see if they can make a match. For older children, add more cards from other parts of Matthew 5–7.

✔ This would be a good time to do an act of kindness for a neighbor!

✔ Have a summer snowball fight. Divide into two teams. Give each team five minutes to crumple colored paper into balls. Signal an additional five minutes for teams to

build their forts with sofa cushions, pillows, etc. On your signal, fire away. Teams may bat away opposing snowballs. Once a paper wad hits the floor, it cannot be recovered. When all snowballs have been flung, count the ones that landed inside the forts. The winners are the ones with most of their color in the opponent's fort. Winners can then require that losers perform in any way they choose, such as singing, dancing, or doing jumping jacks. After the performance announce that winners must do the same stunts!

✔ Inside the word *forgive* is the word *give*. We give someone an undeserved gift when we forgive a sin debt. Play any kind of board game that uses money (such as Monopoly) but put several "forgive" cards in the card stack. Any player receiving a "forgive" card may use it on personal debts or for bailing out another player.

✔ Since teddy bears often hear of injustices and lend their furry comfort, declare an official Bear Day. Mix up some Cream of Wheat cereal or other porridge. Read *The Biggest Bear* and *Winnie the Pooh.* Dribble honey on ice cream or make honey cookies. For honey cookies you'll need the following: 1 cup sugar, 1 cup honey, 1 cup butter, ½ teaspoon almond extract, 1 teaspoon baking soda, 2 tablespoons hot water, 4 cups flour, 1 teaspoon cinnamon, ½ teaspoon cardamom. Mix the baking soda in the hot water. Mix in sugar, honey, butter, and almond extract until smooth. Then add the rest of the ingredients. Store dough in the refrigerator at least one day. Roll out the dough in a very thin circle. Use a bear-shaped cookie cutter to cut cookies. Bake at 350 degrees until brown. (This is an old German recipe from my husband's great-grandmother!)

What mattered most to you during this family time? Talk about it. Use those thoughts in your prayer to Jesus. If you have a grudge against someone because of an injustice, ask Jesus to help you let go of it and give it to Him.

Jesus Quietly Heals People

Stop and Think

The clown came down the center aisle of the church honking her silver horn and waving. The red smile against her white face made everyone grin. When she got to Pastor Rowaldt, he reached to shake her hand. The clown drew back, her mouth shaped like the letter O. She pointed to the big bandage on the back of her hand. Then she cradled her hand and stroked it gently.

"You hurt your hand, I think," said Pastor. The clown nodded and honked her silver horn. "So now you have a bandage on it to protect it."

The clown shook her head. "No?" Pastor looked puzzled. The clown pulled out her magic slate. She wrote, The bandage will heal it.

Pastor read the words out loud. "Do you think bandages heal cuts?" he asked.

The clown honked and nodded happily. The children in the audience began to whisper, and the clown looked out at them with furrowed brows. She took her magic slate over to a little girl named Cynthia in the front row. Cynthia looked uncomfortable because of the attention. The clown pointed to the words on the slate and then raised her eyebrows.

Cynthia shook her head no. The clown tried Nichole, the girl next to Cynthia. Once again she pointed to the words, and

Nichole blushed but shook her head no. The clown scratched her fuzzy red hair and looked at her bandage. She motioned for an older boy, Doug, to stand up and face the audience. She scribbled furiously on her slate, Tell them that bandages heal cuts!

Doug giggled a bit but he finally said, "I can't say that."

The clown lifted her shoulders and raised her hands. Doug understood that she meant, "Why not?" So Doug answered, "Because bandages don't heal things!"

The clown's mouth again formed the letter O. Then staring at her outstretched hand, she walked back to Pastor Rowaldt. He explained, "Bandages cover up cuts so germs don't get in. God made our bodies so wonderfully that special parts inside act like paramedics. Jesus helps our bodies heal. We can't see what's happening under our skin, but Jesus can. That's why we often ask Him to heal people who are sick."

The clown pointed to Pastor Rowaldt and then to the audience. Then she held out her bandaged hand. "Oh, you want us to pray for you?" The clown nodded and honked. So Pastor Rowaldt asked the congregation to fold their hands. He led them in prayer, asking Jesus to help the clown and others who were injured. He invited everyone to stand and say the name of someone in need. If you had been there, who would you have named?

Look and Listen

Jesus heals our bodies so quietly and so often that we usually don't even think about it. Sometimes we think the bandage or the medicine heals us. God has created plants and minerals that contain chemicals and compounds that can help our bodies heal. But Jesus is the main ingredient. Read Mark 1:29–45. What did Simon and Andrew expect Jesus to do? Did He put a bandage on the forehead of Simon's mother-in-law or give her a pain reliever? Once people heard what Jesus did, what did they do? Why couldn't Jesus go into the towns and villages after He healed the man with leprosy?

If you and I could heal people, we might build a hospital and have people line up at the door. Or maybe we'd try healing groups. Why didn't Jesus do that? (See verse 38.) Read Mark 2:1–12. What two "diseases" did Jesus heal? (Paralysis and sin.) What did Jesus preach? (See verses 9–10.) Jesus heals our bodies and souls.

God sighting. Any time you take off a bandage or close a bottle of medicine this week, thank Jesus for healing your body and soul.

Proceed with Care

✔ Make a ring-toss board. Draw the outline of a clown on a piece of poster board or cardboard. Stick pushpins on the ears, nose, tummy, hands, and feet. Decide how many points each one is worth. Use rubber bands, mason jar rings, or the plastic rings from milk container lids for tossing. See how many records you can set!

✔ Check out a fact book on the human body. Cut construction paper to fit the back of a cereal box. Write on the paper interesting facts about our bodies. Use illustrations too. Use a glue stick to attach the paper to the cereal box. You can draw a skeleton and label major bones, or cut out pictures of the digestive system with labels to point out the major organs. We are wonderfully made by God!

✔ Do a shadow operation. Balance a curtain rod with stacks of books on each side. Hang a sheet over the rod and place a table behind the sheet. On the table place such items as a saw, hammer, cardboard screw and screwdriver, cardboard needle with twine attached, a length of knotted stockings, a boot, and anything else that comes to mind.

Backlight the sheet with a bare lamp. The rest of the room should be dark. Then lay the patient on the table, saw the patient as if making an incision, and dramatically yank out various items, such as the stockings and boot. Try to hammer the incision closed, then try the screw, and finally sew it shut. See who can perform the funniest skit.

✔ Make composite bodies. Give every family member a piece of paper. Direct each person to draw a head with a hat on it. Everyone then folds the head out of view and hands his or her drawing to the person on his or her right. Now ask everybody to draw a neck and shoulders. Fold these drawings like before and pass them to the next person. Continue with the arms and torso, and then the legs and feet. Now unfold and see what you have. Do you recognize anyone?

✔ Play Last Letter Chain. Decide on a category, such as "body parts." If the leader says "hair," the next person has to come up with a word that starts with the final consonant or vowel sound of that word. A good response would be "rib." Then the next person could say "bone." Thank God for all our wonderful body parts.

✔ Ask your pharmacist for about 20 empty pill capsules and a blank pill bottle. Write 20 Bible verses that refer to Jesus as the Healer on 20 narrow strips of paper. (Look under "sickness," "disease," and "weakness" in your Bible's concordance.) Roll each strip of paper tightly around a toothpick and insert one into each capsule. When the paper is in place, secure the top of the capsule. Put all 20 capsules into the pill bottle and label it "Medication for the Soul." Give the pill bottle to your pastor for a shut-in member or keep it in your medicine cabinet for your family to use.

✔ Put together an emergency medical kit for the car. Explain to your children what each item is used for. Rent an emergency medical care video from your library. What did it leave out? Praying for the injured person!

Go in Peace

Can you remember how many places on your body have been cut or injured? Now double the number (for injuries you forgot). Add everyone's numbers to show how many times Jesus has healed your family. How many thank yous is that? Sit in a circle on the floor of your living room with your feet pointing to the center of the circle. Thank Jesus for healing your legs. Have the group point their arms toward the center and thank Him again. Tilt your heads inward and thank Jesus for healing all of you, body and soul.

God Can Manage Our Emotions

Stop and Think

Ashley lay very still under the covers. Something dark and horrid was slumped by the closet. She couldn't call her mother; she was too scared. With every tiny sound it moved closer to her bed. Ashley's hands shook, and she could hardly breathe. Just then she saw a shadow pass by her door, and the bathroom light came on. The light was just enough to illuminate her room, enough to see that the dark beast was really her robe hung over the top edge of the closet door. Ashley's heart stopped pounding. She remembered throwing it there before she got in bed.

The light clicked off, and Dad's head popped into her doorway. Mr. Dean usually checked on his two children while they slept. Ashley's eyes were wide open.

"Ashley, you're still awake?"

"Daddy, I was so scared just now. I thought I saw a monster, but it was just my dumb robe."

Mr. Dean glanced at the robe draped over the closet door. "Why didn't you call me?"

"My voice wouldn't work."

"Why didn't you pray to God, then?"

Ashley hadn't thought of that. She would have felt pretty funny asking God to protect her from a robe! Then again, she didn't know it was a robe at the time.

Mr. Dean sat on the edge of the bed. "Did you know that God can take fear out of our hearts? He can! There's a Bible story that tells us all about it."

Look and Listen

Long before Jesus was born, the people of Israel worshiped a fat-bellied god called Baal. Because the Israelites rejected the true God, He allowed the Midianites to overrun them. The Israelites tried to grow their crops but the Midianites would trample the harvest with their camels. One day an Israelite named Gideon hid inside a winepress to thresh wheat so the Midianites wouldn't take the wheat away.

The Angel of the Lord appeared to Gideon and told him God had heard the pleas of His people for help. God said Gideon would lead an army to defeat the Midianites.

"But my clan is the weakest, and I'm the least in my family," Gideon blurted.

"I will be with you!" was the reply.

Now, Gideon wasn't sure. After all, leading an army wasn't something he'd ever thought of doing. "Give me a sign that it's really You," Gideon said. He prepared meat and flat bread and placed them on a rock. Fire came from nowhere and

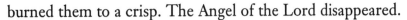

burned them to a crisp. The Angel of the Lord disappeared.

That day God told Gideon to tear down the Baal altar and build one to the true God. Gideon obeyed. He was afraid to build an altar in daylight so he built it the next night. When the townspeople found out, they tried to kill Gideon. But his father wisely said, "If Baal is a real god, let Baal take vengeance on Gideon."

Of course, nothing happened to Gideon because Baal was just a stone with a big belly! Gideon got nervous about the army, so he prayed to God, "If You will give us the victory, show me by making this wool fleece wet and the ground dry." The next morning, Gideon wrung out a bowl full of dew from the fleece, but the ground was dry. Perhaps Gideon thought it might be just a coincidence because he asked God, "Don't be angry with me. Please let me make one more request—make the fleece dry and the ground wet." The next day it was just as he'd asked.

Early in the morning Gideon gathered his soldiers at the spring. God told Gideon there were too many soldiers, so Gideon told everyone who was afraid to leave. Twenty-two thousand left! Imagine Gideon's dismay when only 10,000 remained. They were vastly outnumbered! Then God said that He only wanted the men who drank water while standing, not kneeling. Now Gideon had only 300 men!

Then God showed Gideon a sign he didn't ask for. He said, "If you are afraid to attack, sneak into the enemy camp and listen. Then you will feel bolder."

So Gideon snuck into camp and heard one Midianite say to another, "I had a dream that an enormous bread roll tumbled into our camp and flattened the tent."

His friend answered, "God must be planning to give Gideon the victory."

Gideon felt much encouraged and immediately sent the 300 men to form a ring around the Midianite camp. On Gideon's signal they smashed clay containers that held lit torches. A ring of fire seemed to appear out of nowhere. At the same time, all the men blew ram's horns and shouted, "A sword for the LORD and for Gideon!" This set the Midianites in such a panic that they attacked one another! The remaining Midianite army fled in full retreat. Gideon's army defeated the Midianites, just as God had said.

You can read all the details of this amazing victory in Judges 6 and 7. God didn't remove all of Gideon's fear at once; He continued to show Gideon that He is truthful. Gradually Gideon's courage grew and his fear decreased. God does this for us too.

God sighting. Did you used to be afraid of something like lightning, dogs, dark basements, spiders, or heights? Are you still afraid? If so, ask God to help you feel less afraid. Jesus eased His disciples' anxieties the night before He died. He was struggling then too, but He knew that He had to die in order to save us from death. Watch how He helps you with your fear this week.

Proceed with Care

✔ In Mexico, people make a Christmas ornament called "God's Eye." Lash or glue two craft sticks together into a cross shape. Wrap a colored piece of yarn over and under the cross as illustrated. Change colors by tying on a different colored piece of yarn. These "God's Eyes" remind us that God is always watching over us—day or night. Save the ornaments for your Christmas tree.

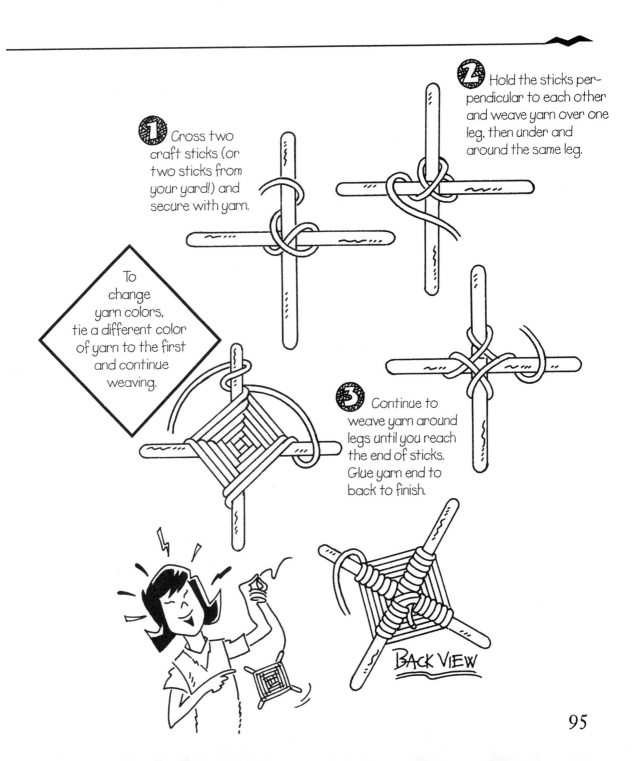

1 Cross two craft sticks (or two sticks from your yard!) and secure with yarn.

2 Hold the sticks perpendicular to each other and weave yarn over one leg, then under and around the same leg.

To change yarn colors, tie a different color of yarn to the first and continue weaving.

3 Continue to weave yarn around legs until you reach the end of sticks. Glue yarn end to back to finish.

BACK VIEW

95

✔ Play Bible Pictionary with the following words from today's story: *wheat, Baal, fleece, kneel, dream, torch, horn,* and *fear*. Divide your family into two teams. Give the one team a minute to guess what word their teammate is drawing. They get a point if they guess the word. If not, the other team may call out one guess. If correct, the point is theirs. Then the other team gets a turn.

✔ We don't have ram's horns, but we can make a kazoo! Punch a hole about one inch from the end of an empty toilet paper roll. Put a square of waxed paper over the end closest to the hole and secure it with a rubber band. Press the other end against your mouth, and hum! What do you think 300 kazoos would have sounded like?

✔ Lie down outside and look at cloud shapes. Sometimes fear is like a cloud monster. It seems so large hanging over us, but then it just blows away.

✔ Drop blobs of leftover paint along a crease of folded paper. Fold the paper closed. Press the paper with your hand, starting at the fold and working outward. Now open the paper. What shapes did you get? Do any look like fear? anger? joy? disappointment?

Substitute your names in Isaiah 41:10 in the appropriate places: "So do not fear, for I am with *Ashley* .... I will strengthen *Ashley* and help *her;* I will uphold *Ashley* with My righteous right hand." Thank God for taking away our fears and giving us everlasting life.

Go in Peace

God Can Bring Good Out of Bad Times

Stop and Think

There is an old Chinese story about a farmer who took a different view of events. One day his horse broke down a fence and raced to freedom in the hills. "So sorry," said the neighbors, "such bad *joss* (luck). You have no horse now."

"It may not be as you think," said the old Chinese farmer. "Who can say what will be?"

That night the horse returned to the corral leading 10 wild stallions. The farmer's son, hearing the noise, jumped up from his pallet and saw all the fine horses. He quickly lodged a board over the broken part of the fence, trapping them. Now the farmer had 11 horses!

"What good *joss!*" cried his neighbors who came to see the fine stallions.

The old Chinese man answered, "It may not be as you think. Who can say what will be?"

The farmer's son began training the wild horses. One of the more testy horses threw the son off. He fell at an odd angle and broke his leg. Word spread quickly in the small territory, and the neighbors gathered to console the father.

"What bad *joss!*"

The wise old man stroked his white beard and answered, "It may not be as you think. Who can say what will be?"

The neighbors wagged their beards and called the farmer an old fool. How can anything good come from such misfortune? The son would be months mending, and the farmer had no hired help.

A few days later a fierce Chinese warlord galloped into the territory with his band of rough fighters. He conscripted every able-bodied young man in the entire area. When the dust settled from their whiplash tour through the region, only one young man remained—because he had a broken leg. None of those men taken ever returned because the warlord's army was defeated.

Years later, the wise old Chinese man sat in the shade of a ginkgo tree, watching his son teach his 6-year-old grandson how to ride. He chuckled to himself, "Who can say what will be?"

Look and Listen

Remember how David killed Goliath with a slingshot? After that, David fell on hard times. King Saul was jealous of David because people treated him like a superstar. King Saul even aimed a spear at David! David went on the run to stay ahead of Saul and his henchmen. David became a fugitive.

Everywhere David went, Saul found him and tried to kill him. Once when David was in Gath, he had to pretend to be insane in order to escape! Read the story in 1 Samuel 22:10–15.

Another time Saul was right around the corner of a mountain with his army, ready to trap David. But God sent a message to Saul that a foreign army was attacking back at home. David escaped. That story is in 1 Samuel 23:24–29.

The old Chinese neighbors would have said, "Bad *joss* indeed." But during David's years of running, he learned all about the land he would soon rule over. He learned about leadership as God sent more and more men to join his company. Just before King Saul died, David had 600 men in his army. So despite the 15 years of hardship, David reaped God's blessings in the end.

God does this in our lives too. The Bible says, "In all things God works for the good of those who love Him, who have been called according to His purpose" (Romans 8:28). We often don't see things that way.

We usually only see the past with 20–20 vision. We can see how God prepared everything to work out for our good. God can even turn evil around for good. We can trust Him to keep the promise of Romans 8.

God sighting. Whenever you pass a shop that sells eyeglasses remember how God helped you with something in your past, even though you didn't see it then.

Proceed with Care

- ✔ Joni Eareckson Tada has books and tapes that chronicle her ministry. She felt God's hand in her life only after she had an accident that left her a quadraplegic. Such true stories of God's support in our lives teach children about real-life heroes. Read some of those stories together.

- ✔ Play Something Good from Something Bad. Ask such questions as: What good can come from the fire alarm going off in the middle of the night? running out of gas? breaking an arm? getting a poor grade? being in the hospital?

- ✔ Life has easy and hard times. Draw a road on a paper plate with straight, wide sections and twisted, narrow sections. Add tunnels if you wish. Bend a paper clip into a flat spiral with pliers and place it on the start. Use a magnet under the plate to get your "traveler" to the heavenly castle at the end.

- ✔ Household jobs may not be fun, but they have their rewards. Make a Job Jar. Write small jobs on slips of paper and put them in a large glass jar. Here are some good jobs for little hands: wash the fingerprints from all the switch plates, clean the closet floor, wash the mirrors, wash a bike, dust-mop under the beds, feather-dust the tops of all the framed pictures, shine the brass, or clean the frying pan. Attach a money tag to each slip for turn-in to the paymaster or attach redemption tags, such as: "Redeem for one hug," "Good for one ice-cream cone," or "Good for three hours of baby-sitting."

- Play Nose to Nose. Blindfold two people and seat them knee to knee. They must try to touch noses without words or hands. Giggling *is* allowed! Here's a game where losing can be fun!

- Nursing homes can be marvelous places if they are run by caring, active staffs that involve the community. Other nursing homes can be places of loneliness and neglect. Be a bright spot in someone's life by planning a monthly visit with a resident who doesn't have many visitors. Plan a sing-along. Learn and play a card game together. Bring materials for a simple craft and make something the person can hang in his or her room. Share your family on one visit. Look at a magazine together. Visits don't have to be long—30 minutes is plenty. Take time to give time.

Let each family member pick a note to hum. Once everyone has a picked a note, ask each person to sing "la." It probably doesn't sound too good! Keep singing "la," but vary your notes slightly until everyone's "la" sounds harmonious. This is what God does with our lives. Praise Him by singing, "We praise You, O Lord, for Your mighty power" while still harmonizing. Ask for suggestions for new stanzas.

Go in Peace

Jesus Does Miraculous Things

Stop and Think

The Sunday school Easter event that year was like no other. All the Holy Week events from Palm Sunday to Easter were going to be filmed. The director and her co-director would have 90 children from the church in costume for this occasion. They had permission to use various buildings at the local college and city hall. Police barricades would block the road as well as a section of a local park for the triumphal entry.

The director seemed distracted as Saturday's filming approached. She prayed every day. "How are we supposed to manage the triumphal entry scene without a donkey, God? We've got the palm branches, the kids in costumes, the cameraman, the permission from the city—even the newspaper people will be there. The big event—and no donkey! You know, Lord, when You needed a donkey, You just asked a favor of a friend nearby. It's not so easy these days. Nobody has donkeys in suburbia!" The woman sighed and put her hands in her lap. After a few moments she said, "Lord, this is Your production. Will You send us a donkey?"

That evening the director phoned the father of one of the children. He had made the crosses for the crucifixion scene. "They're all done," he said. "So, is everything else ready?" he asked.

"We still don't have a donkey," the director sighed.

"Hmm. Wait a minute. Would a Shetland pony do? Let me call you back."

Ten minutes later, the director's phone rang. "Lady, you've got your pony. He'll make a fine donkey."

But Friday morning when the director picked up the palm branches, the florist said, "They say thunderstorms tomorrow."

Confidently the director replied, "It can't rain. Ninety kids will be outside half the day."

She woke up Saturday morning to the patter of rain. "God," she prayed, "Please don't let it rain today! We can't reschedule all this!"

With trepidation the director drove to the church, praying all the way. Her co-director waved to her from the church doorway. "We better start calling people," he called.

"No! No phone calls! The rain is going to stop!" the director insisted as she shook off her umbrella.

A few questioning families began arriving in the drizzle for the first scene.

"Are we still doing it?"

"Yes! Get into costume. We start with the temple scene over at the college. Meet you there!"

The director pleaded with God as she walked toward the front door. "Lord, we have 10 minutes until the first shoot. The rain has to stop. Surely You didn't get us that donkey for nothing."

Eventually, both directors were caught up in the filming. Neither of them gave much thought to the weather. Actually, the overcast sky was perfect for Peter's denial scene in the courtroom parking lot. The triumphal entry was packed not only with the children but also with many onlookers. It looked and felt much like a crowded city. The sun broke through just at that time.

The final shoot of the Passover meal was scheduled for inside the building. As they drove back to the church, the sky opened up and rain started pouring from the sky. It was as if God had put a giant umbrella over the city for five hours and had just removed it. No one could miss the miracle!

Look and Listen

Among His many miracles, Jesus stilled a storm, healed the sick, sent thousands of fish into a net, fed thousands of people with very little food, walked on the sea, and brought dead people to life again. The apostle John tells us that Jesus did many more miracles that aren't recorded in the Bible (John 20:30). Why did Jesus perform miracles? Find out in John 20:31.

Many people believe Jesus was a good person like Mohammad, Gandhi, or Mother Teresa. None of these people ever claimed to be God's Son, though. Read what Jesus says of His ability to do miracles in John 14:10–11.

If you read through verse 14, you'll see that Jesus is still doing miracles, even by request! He certainly did for the director in today's story! Does this mean you can ask for your own private money tree or that everyone would suddenly see you as the world's greatest athlete? Do you see those words "in My name" in verse 14? Do you think Jesus would ask His Father for a money tree or a certain body? No! What would Jesus ask for? (He would pray for help choosing the 12 disciples, for guidance, for power to heal, for protection for Peter against Satan, and for God to forgive His executioners.)

God sighting. The only way to see miracles is to be a God-watcher. It's easier to watch when you're looking for something specific. Pray for something specific in Jesus' name as described above. Then ask God to help keep you alert. Then watch.

Proceed with Care

✔ Play Bible Dice. Divide the family into two teams. Roll the die and name what the number requires: 1–Bible male, 2–Bible female, 3–Bible object, 4–Bible verse (quote the words), 5–book of the Bible, and 6–miracle. Keep a list of each correct answer. No repeats allowed.

- Help the children distinguish magic from miracles. Here is a simple magic trick. Peel a hard-boiled egg. Place the egg on top of a glass jar whose opening is slightly smaller than the circumference of the egg. (Try an olive jar.) Cover the jar with a loose cloth and ask a child to lift up the egg and close his or her eyes. Drop a lit match into the container. Quickly cap it with the egg again and let the cover drop around the container bottom, blocking the view of the match. Have the child open his or her eyes. The egg will be sucked into the container. Explain that only God can perform miracles. Show your child the burnt-out match. Magic always has a trick to it.

- Thread a 30″ string through a button that has two holes. Tie the ends, forming one continuous loop. Now glue two small V-shaped wedges of cardboard facing each other on the same side of the button. Let dry. Hold an end of the string in each hand with the button in the center. Swing it clockwise. Then quickly pull the two ends of the string apart. This will cause the button to rapidly untwist and force your hands together. Pull your hands apart again reversing the twist. Repeat this again and again in rhythm, and the toy will start humming.

Miracles are all around you. A seed that can send its stem up and its roots down no matter how the seed lays in the soil is a miracle. A penguin returning to its original nesting site after a year away is a miracle. Six quintillion (6 with 18 zeros after it) electrons pass through a 100-watt light bulb every second—that's miraculous. It's only the unusual miracles that we pay any attention to—sick people suddenly becoming well or strangers showing up to help and then suddenly disappearing. Thank God for *all* His miracles—including the life He gave up for us.

Go in Peace

God Rested on the Seventh Day

Stop and Think

The white tablecloth for Saturday supper still covers Mama's table even though I have my own home now. I remember carrying the two candles from the living room mantle and setting them carefully in the center of all that whiteness. Mama never used any other tablecloth on Saturday night in all the years I can remember. She said, "White reminds us that God is pure and good. He comes to simple people in a simple way."

We always had fresh French bread at those Saturday suppers. The rest of the week we ate whole wheat bread, but on Saturday the smell of that long loaf spread with the golden butter drew everybody toward the kitchen. French bread will always make me think of Sabbath Eve.

Mama and Papa lit the candles and blessed us before we started eating. One time Mama asked God to help my hair grow. The week before I'd leaned over my birthday candles and caught my long hair on fire! It had to be cut short to even it out, and I cried all week. I remember when Papa asked God to be with my brother during his first time at camp and to bless him with a friend. Doug still remembers meeting Brian there.

We read the Bible every night after supper, but on Sabbath Eve, Papa always read Sunday's sermon text. Then we sang a hymn that one of us had picked. I learned a lot of hymns that way.

Mama left the white tablecloth on the table for Sunday morning. She'd set a white place mat over any spills from the night before. I understood how God makes our hearts clean from sin's stains. Mama said He "bleached" it out.

Papa always made Sunday breakfast—crepes. He'd swirl the batter around the sides of a big, hot pan, and we'd watch the yellow mixture turn crinkly on the edges. He'd flip one deftly onto a plate and set it in front of whoever needed one. I always put raspberry jam down the center line of mine and rolled it up. On special Sundays, Papa put whipped cream on the table for spreading on top of the crepes. I loved to watch the cream melt into white syrup. Yum.

Even though Mama dressed first and ate last, she usually finished about the same time we did. She always wore perfume on Sundays, and whenever I smell that fragrance, I feel like I'm 9 years old again.

We toted our church bags inside the building. Every week one of us got to choose where we'd sit. Mama wore white gloves, and I used to try to keep my hands still like she did. When she noticed, she'd say, "Elizabeth Ann, you're such a lady!" My little brother played with the stuff in his church bag until the sermon. Then he could only color and look at the picture books. I could sing along with the hymns, so I only used my church bag during the sermon. I'd read another bit of whatever book was in my bag. I remember one time the pastor's sermon mentioned C. S. Lewis, and I was in the middle of *The Lion, the Witch, and the Wardrobe!* Eventually I was old enough to listen like my parents did.

Whenever my brother and I both stayed quiet during the sermon (if you didn't, you sat for a half hour on the piano bench when you got home), Papa stopped to pick up doughnuts. We ate them with spicy tea over the white tablecloth. Then the tablecloth vanished until the next Sabbath Eve.

Mama gave me a white tablecloth on my wedding day. Someday one of my children will tell its story too.

Look and Listen

Work can be enormously satisfying. God felt this satisfaction too. Read Genesis 1:31–2:3. But we can fall into extremes when it comes to work. Some of us refuse to strain and sweat and struggle so we never feel the satisfaction of a job well done. God labeled this attitude "sloth." Some of us strive too often, taking on too many hard tasks without a break. Gaining satisfaction through work alone displaces God in our lives and puts us out of balance. So God gave the commandment: "Remember the Sabbath Day and keep it holy." We know that Jesus rested on the Sabbath or seventh day (Luke 4:16) and that Christians are to keep the regular practice of church worship (Hebrews 4:9–10). For Jesus, Sabbath started at sundown on what is now Friday evening. Sabbath lights burned on a white cloth set with two loaves of braided white bread. Jesus received His parents' blessing prayer. After the meal Joseph probably read from a scroll, or they went to the village circle where men shared news of the day, quoted Scripture, and told stories like David's fight with Goliath.

Sabbath morning Jesus and Joseph sat in the front of the synagogue while Mary sat in back with the women. The rabbi began, "Hear, O Israel: The LORD our God, the LORD is one!" (Deuteronomy 6:4) The Shema was then recited by all from Deuteronomy 6:5. Bible readings followed, and the rabbi or a guest spoke a short sermon. (See one Jesus gave in Luke 4.) A discussion followed, then psalms were sung, and a final benediction blessing was given.

No work was done by anyone during Sabbath. The meal of the day was prepared the day before so the women could rest on the Sabbath too. In the afternoon families went for walks, played, told stories, and visited with neighbors. Sabbath ended at sundown with various blessings and the passing of a special box of spices to let the "sweet Sabbath linger" until next week.

God sighting. Prepare for your church worship time by
- asking for forgiveness if there is anyone you have harmed or left unforgiven;

- asking God to bless the musicians, ushers, and speakers with His words;

- praying for "ears that hear";

- requesting the Spirit's zeal to praise wholeheartedly; and

- asking for unity and peace in your congregation.

Then see how you experience worship when you have prepared your hearts like this!

 **Proceed with Care**

- The traditional Sabbath blessing is, "May God bless you and keep you. May God watch over you in kindness. May God grant you a life of good health, joy, and peace." Study the blessings found in Numbers 6:23–26; Romans 15:5–6; 2 Peter 1:2; Jude 24–25; 1 Thessalonians 5:23; Hebrews 13:20–21; and 1 Corinthians 16:23. What parts do each of you like best? Compose your own blessing for the Sabbath. Consider buying a calligraphy kit and learning to write your names. Then write your blessing in calligraphy, cover it with clear vinyl adhesive paper, and use it as a place mat.

- Make spice potpourri together. Mix the following and place in a covered dish: 1 tablespoon crushed anise, 5 sticks of cinnamon, 1 tablespoon crushed allspice, ¼ cup whole cloves, 6 broken nutmegs, 3 broken vanilla beans, 1 tablespoon ginger, 1 cup coarse salt (not iodized).

- Use a thin brush or cotton-tipped swab to paint liquid bleach on construction paper. The color disappears but leaves white lines that can be very pretty. (Remind your children not to do this craft without your supervision.) Draw hearts on the construction paper and paint them with the bleach. God makes our hearts clean when we ask for His forgiveness!

Make French bread together. Dissolve 1 package yeast in 1¼ cups lukewarm water. Let it sit five minutes. Then add 1 tablespoon sugar, 1½ teaspoons salt, and 2 cups flour. Beat until smooth. Add ¾ to 1 cup more flour and knead the dough until it has an elastic consistency. Let it rise in a warm place until it doubles. Punch it down and let it rest 15 minutes. Grease a cookie sheet and sprinkle it with cornmeal. Roll the dough into a 15″ × 10″ rectangle. Roll it up and place it seam side down on the cookie sheet. Make slashes about every two inches. Brush the top with cold water. Let it rise until double again. Bake at 375 degrees for 25 minutes.

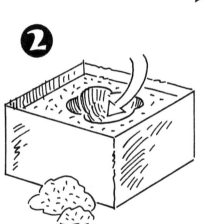

Make a sand candle. Pack damp sand into a large bowl or box and shape a depression two to six inches deep. Attach one end of a strong cotton string to a metal washer and tie the other end to a stick. Lay this stick across the top of the bowl or box, centering it over the sand as illustrated. The string should be taut. Pour melted paraffin wax into the depression. Cool several days. Lift out the candle and brush off loose sand. Vary your candles by coloring the sand or the paraffin or changing the shape.

What do you do that shows how much you love Mom or Dad? (You like to spend time with them, try to please them, try to do what they desire, like to hear others praise them, enjoy giving them gifts, and want their comfort when you are troubled.) What do you do that shows God how much you love Him? (You like to spend time with Him in prayer and in reading His Word, try to please Him by doing what He says is right, like to hear others speak well of Him and sing praises to Him, enjoy giving Him gifts, and want to be with Him when you are troubled.) Our love for God grows as we interact with Him. Write a letter to God. Tell Him how much you love Him and why. Put the date on your letter. Consider keeping a journal every Sunday to help "keep the day holy."

Go in Peace

Jesus Reaches Out as a Friend to All

What should I do? Megan wondered. Jenny had grabbed her arm a few minutes ago on the playground and pulled her toward the big pine tree on the side. She had guessed what came next. "I'm not talking to Hoi Kee today. She didn't call me last night to talk about math. So I'll be *your* friend today, Megan! Let's sit here and tell secrets. That'll make Hoi Kee mad!"

Jenny scrunched down on the scrubby grass below the tree trunk. Slivers of sunlight penetrated the sparse branches, but nothing blocked the cold wind. Some of the brown needles on the ground stuck to Megan's coat as she settled herself.

Why does Jenny only pay attention to me when she's fighting with Hoi Kee? Megan wondered. Still, I like Jenny, and I

Stop and Think

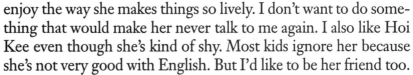

enjoy the way she makes things so lively. I don't want to do something that would make her never talk to me again. I also like Hoi Kee even though she's kind of shy. Most kids ignore her because she's not very good with English. But I'd like to be her friend too.

Just then Hoi Kee came out of the school door and began walking toward the swings. She hadn't seen the two under the tree yet. She sat on an empty swing, her back toward the girls.

"This won't work," Jenny said aloud. She turned her head and flashed Megan a knowing smile. "I'm thirsty. Let's get a drink." As quick as that she jumped up and began moving toward the water fountain by the building in front of the swings.

Megan got up a bit slower and dusted off the back of her coat. Jenny had stopped near enough to the swings to be heard and called, "Megan! Come on!"

Megan glanced over just as Hoi Kee turned toward Jenny's voice. Slipping off the swing, Hoi Kee began walking toward Jenny.

"You here! I wondered where you are!"

But Jenny turned her back and urged Megan, "Hurry up, Slowpoke." Megan stuffed her hands into her coat pockets and headed toward Jenny. Hoi Kee and Megan got to her at the same time.

"So, now what we do?" Hoi Kee asked brightly.

"Whatever it is, it doesn't include you!" Jenny smirked. Hoi Kee backed up a step, a stunned look on her face. Then she pursed her lips and put her hands on her hips.

"Jenny, what this about? We friends."

"All right, Miss Smarty, how come you didn't call me yesterday after school like I told you to?"

"Brother on phone. I go with Father," Hoi Kee explained.

"Guess you just don't have time for me anymore then," Jenny quipped. "Come on Megan. We're thirsty. We're getting a drink."

Look up Luke 7:36–50 in your Bible. Then discuss these questions: What did the woman do? What do you think of her? What did Simon do? What do you think of Simon?

The really interesting part of this story is Jesus' reaction. If you were a guest at someone's home and he didn't bother to greet you and then talked under his breath about you, would you stay? I would have told Simon how rude he was, helped the woman up, and gone over to her house! On the other hand, Simon was an important man in the group. Maybe I would have wanted to stay on his good side so I would have moved my chair away from the woman Simon didn't like.

But Jesus didn't do either of those things. Instead He told Simon a story. Jesus wanted Simon to realize that he also had done bad things. The woman wasn't the only sinner in the room. If Simon listened to Jesus' story and then thought about how rude he'd been, he might have figured out that he was being bossy and proud—just like Jenny. Megan wanted to be a friend to both girls. Jesus wanted to be a friend to both the woman and Simon.

Jesus wants to be a friend to everyone—bossy people, shy people, kind people, and mean people. Sinners can't change for the better unless Jesus comes into their hearts to work from the inside.

God sighting. When you see someone being bossy or mean this week, ask Jesus to be his or her friend. How might Jesus use you to do that? (Whenever God puts someone you've just prayed for into your path, you know He's ready to help you love that person. Try it!)

Proceed with Care

- Play Alike and Different. Put 10 objects on the table, such as a spoon, a toy, soap, a watch, etc. It doesn't matter what they are. Pick up any two objects and ask, "How are these two different?" That's the easy question. Then ask, "How are these two alike?" (They have the same shape, size, or function; they start with the same letter; or they are made of the same material.) After playing several rounds, point to two family members. Ask: How are they alike? different? How are the woman and Simon alike and different?

- Plan a progressive dinner. Decide on three other families who might enjoy a caravan. Then decide whether your family would prefer to do appetizers, soup/salad, sandwiches, or dessert. Figure out who will help make your part of the meal. What toys will be shared at your house? Then pick a couple of possible dates and make the phone calls.

- Roleplay some situations where one person needs to confront the other. Don't allow any name-calling or character judgments; stick to the issues. Look at how Jesus did this in Luke 7:44–46. Here are some situations: Mom is once again picking up the coat her son dropped on the floor. Brother has again barged into sister's room without knocking. One sister is playing with the other sister's toy without asking. Son is watching TV, but Dad sees homework that isn't finished. Add some of your own. For extra insight, let the children play parent parts and vice versa!

- Make a family prayer ball. Trace a lid or some other circular object on 20 pieces of stiff paper. Cut the circles out of the paper. Use a ruler to draw a triangle on each one, points touching the circumference. Mom or Dad can score the lines with one point of the scissors so that they will fold up sharply. Decide on 20 people who need your prayers this week. Include people such as the president of

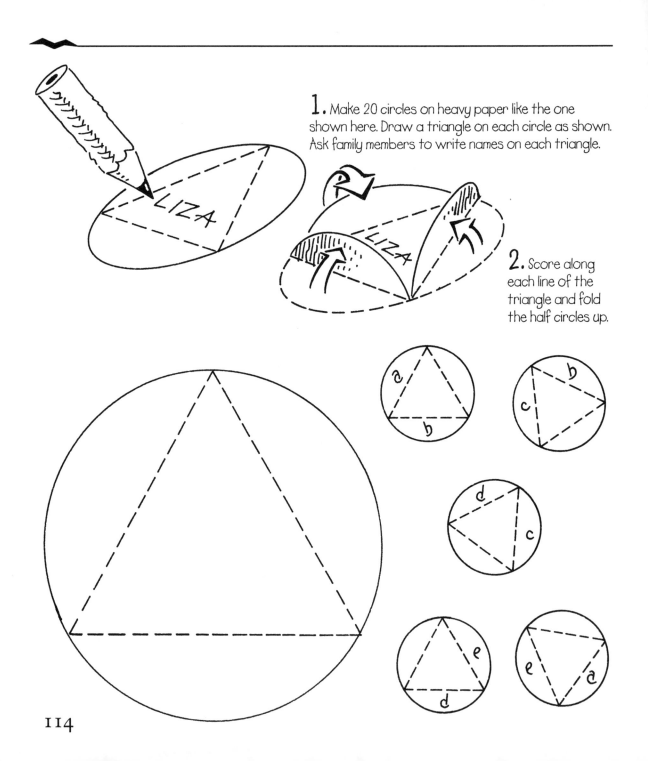

1. Make 20 circles on heavy paper like the one shown here. Draw a triangle on each circle as shown. Ask family members to write names on each triangle.

2. Score along each line of the triangle and fold the half circles up.

the United States, your pastor, and your loved ones as well as those whose behavior limits their number of friends. Tape or staple the folded edges of 10 of the triangles (name side up) to make the top of the ball. Do the same for the bottom. Then fit the two halves together to complete the ball. Whenever you want to pray for someone listed on the ball, drop it and see whose name is on the bottom. Pray for that person.

Go in Peace

When we pray, "God bless _____," we're asking God to give that person many wonderful gifts, such as smiles, kind words, closeness to God, peaceful sleep, uplifting music, and the desires of his or her heart. Stand in a circle and ask God to bless the person on your right. You might put your hand on his or her head when you do this. Thank God for that family member and for His Son, Jesus, who loves us equally and so much that He gave us the ultimate gift—His life.

God Has Plans for Us

Stop and Think

Brian plopped down on the porch step, his chin on his hand. An ant raced past on the sidewalk by his foot. He picked up a stick lying there and poked at a crack where the ant had gone. The ant didn't come out. "Not even ants to play with," Brian mumbled.

After some minutes, he tossed the stick toward the street where his bike lay in the grass.

Sure, I can ride my bike, but there's nobody to ride with, he thought. Back home I'd be next door at Greg's house. We'd play with the stuff he got on his birthday. There's nothing to do here. All the neighbors around are old people or teenagers.

Mom came out of the house with two Popsicle treats. She sat down next to Brian and held out one.

"A January Popsicle," she said smiling. Brian took it without a word and looked again for the ant. Mom sat quietly, gazing out over the flowering shrubs of their new house. "You don't get flowers in winter back home," she said.

"You don't get boring neighbors and a dumb school either. I bet these boys don't even know who the Chicago Cubs are," answered Brian.

"You sound bored," Mom said.

"I *am* bored," Brian said. "I never wanted to come here. I liked our old house and my friends. There was lots of stuff to do there."

"And you don't think anything good will be here?"

"No, I don't! Look at the houses right by us. Do any kids live there—no!"

"It doesn't seem possible that you could have friends here," Mom echoed.

Brian turned his head toward Mom. "Mom, I don't like it here." His lip began to quiver.

Mom looked into Brian's face and felt his hurt. She put an arm around his shoulder as Brian leaned toward her. Dear God, she prayed silently. Let me love this boy just as he needs to be loved. Then she sighed and held Brian as tears slipped down his cheeks. Mother and son sat quietly, thinking on the porch step.

Look and Listen

Read 1 Samuel 17:1–50. A shepherd's life can get boring. Young David stayed with his sheep and was often all by himself. He probably spent a lot of hours slinging stones at a target to pass the time. Once he had to fight a bear and a lion! He

probably wondered how he would ever manage! Here's a question for you to think about: What if God had put David into a carpenter's family so that he had lots of company and never had to fight off big, scary animals? What would have happened in the Goliath story then?

David didn't fight that giant until he was older, but God had planned to make sure he was ready. He sent fierce animals to convince David that God would help him against powerful enemies. At just the right time, Goliath challenged Israel, and God had David ready to meet him. Did you know that God has plans for your life too? He is making sure you'll be ready for what's ahead.

David wrote a song about God—Psalm 23. In that psalm David calls God his Shepherd, the One who leads us various places. See if you can find five places David mentions.

See if you can find the phrase "Sometimes You leave me." You didn't find it? David knew that God never leaves us. We can't move away from Him. We can't get left behind. Nobody can suddenly take our place so that He doesn't notice us. He always knows exactly where we are and how we're doing. How can Brian be helped by knowing that God has plans for us and that He prepares us so we're ready for what's ahead?

Pretend you're Brian's mom and explain how God always has plans for us. (Maybe God is getting Brian prepared to handle making new friends for when he goes to college. Maybe God knows Brian needs more time right now to do things with Mom because a new sister is coming and Mom will be busier then.) We can trust God to know how we feel and to be doing good things for us all the time. He can change our attitude about boring times or lonely times when we talk to Him.

God sighting. Can you remember a time when something you learned helped you? What did God have to do with that learning experience? How did He prepare you for that situation?

Proceed with Care

✔ We can learn to have patience during boring or stressful times. Challenge family members to count how many times each says, "I'm being patient," this week. Give one point for every time you say it quietly at the appropriate time. Keep track of the score on the refrigerator. Start now by seeing who can stand silent and still for three minutes. Winners get five points. Next week give a small hourglass as a Most Patient Award.

✔ Play Upside-Down Bible with today's story. Turn your Bible over and retell today's story. Challenge the kids to catch your errors by raising their hands. Then tell the story with wrong bits like "Goliath was a Japanese sumo wrestler"; "David saw Goliath and ran back to hide behind his older brother"; and "David pulled out his sword and fought with Goliath in a fierce battle." Be ready to become more and more outrageous if the kids don't catch your errors!

✔ Draw Goliath's 9' shape with colored chalk on your driveway or back patio. Have everyone lie inside the outline to compare sizes. He was even taller than Dad is! Discuss with your family how David's faith in God's plan helped him beat Goliath.

✔ Assign phrases of Psalm 23 to each family member. Let them illustrate their phrases however they like. Post the entire psalm on the inside of the front door and try memorizing it together. Practice every morning.

✔ Have target practice. Create a sock ball by putting two socks together and rolling them up from the toe end. Fold the cuff of one over both rolled up socks. Set up an empty plastic soda bottle as a target. Put it at whatever distance seems fair. You might draw a frown on the bottle and call out, "Sock-ed ya" when you score. Later, you can "sock" your children with sock balls when they are feeling down until they giggle and let you get close enough for a hug.

Go in Peace

Read the promise God makes in Jeremiah 29:11. Substitute your names in the verse in the appropriate places: "I know the plans I have for *Brian*," declares the LORD, "plans to prosper *Brian* and not to harm *him*, plans to give *Brian* hope and a future." Praise God for planning your lives and preparing you for what's ahead.

God Is Trustworthy

Stop and Think

Sylvia gripped the edge of the desk, startled by the laughter around her. She saw Diane standing at the front of the classroom, poised and confident. Apparently she'd just made a joke, and everyone responded. She always does so well, Sylvia thought. She'll probably get an A on this speech like she does on everything.

Sylvia looked down at her hands and realized she was still clenching the top of her desk. She pulled them back into her lap, glancing around to see if anyone had noticed. Sharon was looking at her, so she forced herself to smile at Sharon. Sharon likes everybody, and everybody likes Sharon, Sylvia thought. Even the boys like her and choose her for soccer at recess.

Sylvia resumed watching Diane who continued her speech about Illinois agriculture. Diane can make anything interesting. Look at the big ear of corn she brought. I don't have any props like that for my speech. She noticed the teacher was nodding and smiling.

Sylvia pushed her left hand across the fabric of her dress. She rubbed her eyebrow. She scratched her head and then crossed her legs the other way. Her stomach flip-flopped. I can't do this, she thought, pushing her speech to the other side of her desk. She stretched her back straight for a second and then let her shoulders droop again. Breathe deeply, she remembered. Deep and slow. She recrossed her legs.

Now everyone was clapping, and Diane began passing out little bags of popcorn to everyone. "My goodness, Diane. We're sure going to remember that Illinois produces corn!" said the teacher.

"She'll get an A. I just know it," Susan whispered to Sylvia.

Sylvia moved her mouth into a smile again, but her stomach was in knots. In seconds the teacher would call on the next person to speak. Every moment seemed a year long. Breathe slow. Breathe slow. Breathe slow!

"Bruce, would you tell us about industry now?"

Sylvia leaned back. Not me, she sighed. She watched Bruce march up to the front. He carefully put his notes on the podium and then paused to make eye contact with the audience. The teacher graded you on that. I'm going to forget to pause, Sylvia thought. She straightened her back again. Her heart returned to a normal beat, but the tension tired her shoulder muscles and neck.

Bruce droned on about printing companies. Sylvia looked around. Then she pulled her speech to the center of the desk and began reading it for the umpteenth time. When she finished the first sheet, she quietly slipped it under the second sheet, moving slowly and looking at Bruce while she did it.

In the middle of the third page, people started clapping again. Sylvia's hand jerked and knocked the pages on the floor.

Now they're out of order! What if I'm next and the pages are out of order!

Tears threatened as she bent over. Bruce passed her, almost stepping on one of her pages.

"Thank you, Bruce," said the teacher. "Now let's hear from … " she checked her class list, "Sylvia Brown."

Look and Listen

Most people struggle with worry. What have you worried about lately? Think of worry like marbles rattling around in a shoebox. You can stop the noise by getting rid of the marbles or wrapping soft cotton wadding all around them. God does the same thing with worry. Sometimes He gets rid of the problem. Other times, He surrounds the worries with His presence—like putting soft cotton wadding in your heart.

Two Bible stories show us what happens when we go to God with our worries. Read Matthew 8:23–27. How did God solve the worry? (He removed it by stopping the storm!)

Now read Matthew 11:1–6. Did Jesus send an angel army to rescue John? No! Instead Jesus reassured and comforted John by letting him know that He was doing exactly what the Messiah does! God gives believers a command in 1 Peter 5:7: "Cast all your anxiety on Him because He cares for you." "Cast" means to throw away from yourself. We fail His command when we gather our worries close to ourselves and they "rattle around" in our hearts.

When we believe in God's love for us, we trust that God will help us with our problems—no matter how small or how big.

God sighting. Ask God to strengthen your trust in His willingness and ability to care for you. Put a marble in a box lined with cotton and put it somewhere where you can get to it easily. Shake the box the next time you're tempted to "get rattled." Give that worry to Jesus; see how He works it out for you!

✔ Stack same-size pieces of paper together and staple them along one side for a homemade notebook. Then draw a marble at the bottom of the last page. Let the second to last page drop over what you just drew. Draw the marble again but a little higher up. Continue flipping down a page and redrawing the marble. About halfway through your stack, begin drawing the marble going back down. When finished, hold the pad near your face and flip through it quickly. Watch the marble "jump."

✔ Blow up a balloon, knot it, and then pop it near the knot. Cut the knot off and stretch the flattened balloon over an empty frozen juice can. Secure the balloon with a rubber band. Put five grains of rice on top of the can and move it near a loud radio. The rice will jump! Sometimes being near commotion makes us edgy too.

✔ Discuss this scene with your family. There was once a traveler carrying a heavy pack. A horse and cart came down the road, and the driver offered the man a lift. The man climbed up to the seat and sat there, the load still bending his back. "Put your pack in the cart, friend!" the driver said. "Oh, no, I couldn't do that. You've already given me a ride!" How is this like people who know they are saved but don't give God their day-to-day problems?

✔ Play Projection. Have each player write or draw three motions, in order, on paper. Then take turns performing the first two motions. The other players have to guess what the next motion will be. If no one can guess, perform the last motion. Keep score for correct guesses. Play until everyone realizes that we aren't too good at projecting what someone will do next. Most of our worries never really come to pass because people almost never react how we expect them to. Remind each other to stop playing projection.

✔ Stand 5–10 feet away from a wastebasket. How many Ping-Pong balls can you *bounce* into the basket? Go for a family record. Don't get rattled!

✔ Play balloon soccer. Sit in a rectangle with a goalie on each end. Each goalie should have a pin. One team sits opposite the other. The goal is to bat the balloon toward the team's goalie who must then pop the balloon. Whoever pops the most balloons wins. When you send your problems to the True Goalie you never see them again!

Go in Peace

What do you think God is trying to say to you through today's Bible verses and stories? Write your thoughts in a journal, then turn them into a prayer, thanking God for taking on your burdens.

God Builds Trust in Us

Stop and Think

"One more! One more!" Sweat beaded Jessie's forehead. He gritted his teeth and lunged. His dusty hand held to the last bar on the jungle gym, and he pulled himself forward. Jessie let himself hang there briefly before he dropped to the dirt below.

"You made it! All 16!" cried Wes.

A slow grin spread across Jessie's face. He looked back at the 16 rungs.

The first time he ever came to this park, some bigger boys goaded him into trying the high jungle gym bars. One of them lifted him to the first rung. No sooner did he try to let go with one hand to reach for the next rung than he flipped sideways to the ground. The big boys laughed and then, one by one, practically catapulted across. Jessie watched from the ground.

Jessie practiced very hard after that day. He'd noticed that people had to sort of swing to get to the next rung. He began the swing and then let go of one hand midway on the swing back. It worked! Nobody was around to see the first triumph, but another kid, Wes, came soon after.

Wes told Jessie about putting dirt on his hands for a better grip. Jessie tried it and managed three bars! Wes never showed off the way the big boys did, even though Wes crossed the bars with ease. "I do it a lot so my muscles are strong," he said once.

After that, Jessie worked on his muscles. He climbed the oak tree by the fence. Mom suddenly had a helper carrying in the groceries. He did chin-ups and push-ups in gym class like never before. He used books for weights on each hand and lifted them before school each morning. Jessie could measure his muscle tone by how many rungs he reached.

It all paid off today. Even the big boys saw his Olympic performance and congratulated him. Antonio clapped him on the back, and Ramirez gave him a thumbs-up. Jessie knew with practice, he'd do those bars as easily as the others.

Look and Listen

Daniel's first faith encounter did not put him face to face with lions! It put him face to face with vegetables! Read Daniel 1. Daniel took a risk by obeying God's dietary commands in this new country. But God proved Himself trust-

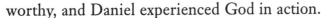

worthy, and Daniel experienced God in action.

The next rung on Daniel's faith ladder was a dream. The king demanded that the wise men not only tell him what his nightmare meant but give a description of the dream to prove the interpretation wasn't made up! None of the other wise men could discover the dream. In a fury, the king ordered all the wise men killed. Daniel risked an audience with the angry king to beg for time. The king gave him one day. Daniel and his three friends prayed earnestly. Once again, God came through for Daniel and told him the dream. Daniel's faith muscles got a bit stronger.

Years later, Daniel watched as this same king built a gold statue 90 feet tall and told everyone to bow down to it. Daniel's three friends refused to disobey God and were tossed into a fiery furnace. Miraculously, the fire did not burn even a hair on their heads! God also builds our trust in Him by showing us how He comes through for others.

The king had another frightening dream and told Daniel to interpret it. Daniel believed God wanted the king to hear the truth. So Daniel told the king that God was displeased with him for trying to be God. Daniel continued, telling the king how God planned to allow the king to become insane until the king repented. The king refused to repent and went insane about a year later. Daniel's faith muscles were growing ever stronger.

The next king to reign was a wicked man who used the temple cups for a drunken party. God caused a hand to appear from nowhere and write strange words on a wall. Everyone was spooked, including the new king. He asked Daniel to read the words. Again, Daniel knew the words were not complimentary, but Daniel knew God wanted him to translate the writing. This new king could easily have ordered Daniel killed. That very night, the young king died.

So Daniel now faced another new king. This king announced that anyone praying to a god other than the king would be thrown into a lions' den. By now God had built up Daniel's faith so that it was at its strongest. Daniel risked being mauled by lions, but he prayed to the true God just as openly as he'd always done. And again—God came through!

God does the same for us. He provides opportunities for us to trust and obey Him. With every experience, our faith muscles grow stronger.

God sighting. This week watch for times that require you to trust in God and not in your own solutions. What did you risk?

Proceed with Care

✔ Draw pictures of yourselves while you have paper grocery bags over your heads. Take the bags off. We really aren't very good at seeing things clearly when we're in the dark. When we're facing trouble and can't see the future, it's best to get some light from Jesus by praying. He can help us draw the right conclusions.

✔ Exercise little hand muscles. Give your child five numbered index cards. Can he or she punch the correct number of holes on each card with a hole punch? (Older children can do division and multiplication.) You notice muscles when they're used strenuously!

✔ Visit a nearby park and use it as an obstacle run. Determine the course, for example: (1) swing eight times; (2) climb up the slide ladder and climb back down; (3) climb the ladder again and slide down; (4) race around the merry-go-round twice, once forward and once backwards; (5) lift the teeter-totter six times. This is good for exercising as well as following verbal directions.

- Make a muscle-person salad. Use half a peach for the stomach, carrot sticks for arms, celery sticks for legs, and an apricot half for the head. Add raisin eyes and a pimento mouth. Use halved cherries on the arms for muscles.

- Discuss how you've built trust in each other all your lives. Ask the children to use specific examples to explain how they've learned to trust you. Then share how you, the parents, learned to trust them with various responsibilities and privileges. Finish with the classic trust test: Have each person fall backward into the ready arms of the family. (This is a great experience to refer to when the kids are teenagers.)

- Write a script together for the story of the fiery furnace (Daniel 3). Create the furnace with chairs and sofa pillows. Tape or pin red paper flames to the cushions. Use long bathrobes for costumes. Dress the king in a paper crown and a regal sheet for a cape. Invite neighbor kids for other parts too. Consider asking your neighbor to videotape the production with your camcorder.

Go in Peace

Stack chairs, buckets, books, pots, etc., to make a tower exactly as tall as the tallest person in your family. God builds trust in us little by little, one new experience on top of another. Can you recall times He was building trust in you? Thank Him for those times.

God Defends Us when We're Defenseless

Stop and Think

The eagle flew high over the battlefield, his piercing eyes catching every detail of the tremendous struggle below. The ghoulish army of the Death Knight continued its relentless press against the army of the Red Prince. Thousands stood bravely, resisting the horde of hissing, snakelike griebs, razor-mouthed skikes, and the shimmering glicks.

The eagle noted Sir Martin tightening his belt of truth against a fire-breathing eck. Sir John refastened his breast plate after deflecting a lunge. Princess Joan was everywhere with a bright blade, her shod feet protected from the goo a grieb spewed in her path. Many shields fended off the flaming arrows of the Death Knight. Sir Francis had been lured into removing his helmet briefly by sorrow but now had it firmly in place. Lady Teresa whirled her sword against an onslaught of germ-throwers. The eagle nodded encouragement to each upturned face, instilling each seeking warrior with renewed spirit and strength.

But off on the far edge by the scorched desert lands, a soldier faltered. The eagle caught the motion at once and sped to defend. The shimmering glicks had the soldier surrounded so that at every turn he could only see mirrored images of himself or the fearsome faces of glicks. Every mirror showed the same picture: a man beaten in defeat, worthless, and ashamed. "Look up!" screeched the eagle. "Look at me!" The soldier dropped to one knee as the glicks pressed inward. "Here! Above you!" the eagle screamed again.

With one outstretched wing, the eagle knocked the soldier onto the ground, but in that moment before the glicks could close in entirely, the man looked up—straight into the hovering eagle's face. His eyes locked on that face full of compassion. "You know me," the man gasped. "You know everything! But you love me still!"

"I love you still, my own dear son. You are not merely what the mirrors show you! Look deeply into my eyes. They show the truth."

The soldier gazed steadily while the glicks jabbered trying to distract him. In the eagle's eyes, the man saw himself covered with a red cape, marked with a cross, and filled with a flame of fire in his breast.

With angry snarls, the glicks called in reinforcements to strengthen the glare of their mirrors, hoping to interfere with the soldier's vision. But it was already too late. The Red Prince galloped his white stallion into their midst, and at his battle roar, those who escaped his sword fled wildly.

The eagle hovered just an instant more and then flew to the shoulder of the Red Prince. The fallen fighter rose up as the prince clasped his arm. "Fight on, my brother. Stand your ground! You know now how to resist these!"

"Yes," the man answered as the eagle flew skyward. "I will look up to the eagle. The glicks will not catch me staring at them or their mirrors again!"

Look and Listen

Sometimes we only pay attention to how we botched things in our lives. We become easy prey for darkness and discouragement. God says, "Come to Me, all you who are weary and burdened and I will give you rest" (Matthew 11:30).

A story in the Old Testament shows God keeping this promise to one of His soldiers—a king! Read the story and find out who was trying to destroy this king in 2 Kings 18:17–37.

The first time Hezekiah faced this enemy, he got scared

and gave away all the silver and the gold from the temple (verse 15). But money wasn't going to work again. God wanted King Hezekiah to look to Him. He allowed the Assyrian army to rail against Jerusalem. Once again Sennacherib boasted that he would destroy Jerusalem—with his army. This was no idle threat!

This time Hezekiah cried out to God to save the people. Read his prayer in 2 Kings 19:15–19.

That very night God sent an angel to kill 185,000 enemy soldiers! When the evil leader saw all the dead bodies, he took to his heels. What do you think King Hezekiah learned from this experience?

Is God still the same today? Can He send in an angel to get rid of evil armies if He chooses to? Can He send an angel strong enough to handle your problems? Yes! God is not only good, wise, and strong, He also calls Himself our defender (Isaiah 51:22). Whenever situations become too difficult, God shields us from evil. "[God] will not let you be tempted beyond what you can bear. But when you are tempted, He will also provide a way out so that you can stand up under it" (1 Corinthians 10:13).

Sometimes we would like to be delivered from trouble sooner than God decides. He allows troubles to build long enough to enhance our endurance. God knows exactly when our faith muscles are stretched as far as they can go. At that point, He will deliver, even if it means knocking us flat on our backs so that the only way to look is up! What better way is there to get us in the habit of looking to Him for daily help!

God sighting. Ask someone in your church community, "Can you tell of a time when God rescued you from trouble?" Invite the person to share the story with you and your family personally, in writing, or over the phone. Thank God together for sending us His Son to rescue us from our sins.

✔ Just as the glicks in the story today, Satan likes to make us feel bad about ourselves. We think such things as: *You'll never get this. Just give up. You are so clumsy. They love him or her more because you're so stupid. You can't do anything right. It's all your fault.* Do you ever think like that? Write on paper the phrases that come into your mind. Tear the paper up into tiny pieces and throw it away to remind yourself that you are God's soldier.

✔ Make an army of gingerbread boys and girls. Use icing to add the "full armor of God" as described in Ephesians 6:13–17.

✔ Sketch a family crest in the shape of a shield. Draw a cross as illustrated to divide the shield. In each of the four corners, draw symbols of your family members' character traits that demonstrate God's presence in your family. Write a family motto across the bottom. Post your family crest on the front door this week.

✔ The sword Paul describes in Ephesians 6 is not the long sword people usually think of. This sword is a dagger. A dagger is used for final defense when the enemy is practically on top of you. Paul uses this weapon to stand for God's Word. One reason we memorize verses of God's Word is so we can recall them when we're in trouble. Make several daggers out of paper. On the daggers print Bible verses that you've learned like 1 Corinthians 10:13.

✔ Draw your left hand with your index finger pointing straight and the other fingers curled in. Cut the outline out of the paper. Tie yarn in a bow around the index finger. Write "Prayer Reminder" on one side and "Look Up" on the other. Keep this reminder in a handy spot.

As a family say the words of Ephesians 6:18–20 several times. Promise each other and God that you will "fearlessly make known the mystery of the Gospel."

Pray in the Spirit on all occasions with all kinds of prayers and requests. With this in mind, be alert and always keep on praying for all the saints. Pray also for me, that whenever I open my mouth, words may be given me so that I will fearlessly make known the mystery of the gospel, for which I am an ambassador in chains. Pray that I may declare it fearlessly, as I should (Ephesians 6:18–20).

Go in Peace

Jesus Is a Friend in Lonely Times

Stop and Think

The late afternoon sun inched a finger of light toward the girl huddled in the back of the cave. It was hard to tell how old she was with her knees pulled up to her chest and her arms wrapped around them. If you'd have asked her this morning, she would have straightened up tall and announced, "Eight," with her usual confidence. But not now.

"Hoo!" she called and listened to the echoes bouncing off the walls. "Hah!" she called again. When the echoes stopped, the hush returned.

The sun ray reached her sneaker now. Janey stretched her leg into the light, enjoying the warmth on her jeans. The cave was cool even though it was a hot day. Actually the cave was a large storm sewer pipe running under an old road near her house. Janey never showed it to anyone. It was her secret place. Occasionally a car passed overhead. Whenever she heard the rumble of tires on gravel, she'd think, And they'd never guess I'm here.

Janey stretched out full length along the cement floor, letting the sun touch all of her. She laced her fingers under her head. "April left five days ago. That makes nine more days before she gets back." Janey looked at a crack in the cement ceiling. Its shape reminded her of a friendship bracelet April gave her for her last birthday. "I sure miss April. There's nothing to do. I'm all out of ideas, and I don't want to do the chores. I'm bored, God. There's nobody to play with now but Heather."

The sunlight moved farther back in the cave as Janey lay there recalling episodes with her older sister, Heather—a silly camp song she taught Janey last year, the puppet show Heather

133

got her friends to help with, the time she pulled Janey's shoe out of the mud and helped her home. Janey smiled, recalling Mom's face when both girls came home covered in mud.

"Could a sister be a friend?" Janey wondered. "Heather is way older than me." Janey sat up and crossed her legs. She looked out the entrance and saw two squirrels chasing each other around a tree. "Are you friends?" Janey asked them. One actually stopped and looked around until he saw Janey. Then he came slowly toward her. Janey held her breath. Just then a car crossed overhead and the squirrel dashed away.

Again, Janey asked herself, Who is a friend? "A friend is someone who likes to be by you," Janey decided aloud. "A friend is someone who stays even when others go away." She thought of April last year at school when some of the other girls just walked off without her. April stuck up for her when they teased her about her big feet too. Now that's a friend, thought Janey.

Look and Listen

David and Jonathan are biblical models of friendship. Jonathan, King Saul's son, impresses us with his willingness to be an equal with David, a shepherd's son. He shows no jealousy knowing that God has given David the throne, passing over Jonathan's birthright. In fact, the very last time the two friends saw each other, Jonathan encouraged David. Read the conversation in 1 Samuel 23:15–19.

A friend helps someone "find strength in God." That means helping someone in trouble, like David, remember that God is love. A friend will remind you that God has a plan for your life. God has compassion for you and forgives you. He made you.

A friend prays with you and for you. Jesus is your friend too. He comes to you, seeking you out. Remember the Bible story of the shepherd going after the lost lamb? He kept looking until he found that one lamb. Jesus keeps coming for you too; He wants you near Him. Friends are like that.

Jesus helps us find strength. If life were only full of good times, we'd never need to be strong. We'd never learn to be courageous. We'd never be called to sacrifice. The qualities of endurance, helpfulness, and kindness could never thrive without hard times. God can even turn evil back on itself so that it does not destroy us but provides us with opportunities to develop character. Jesus stands as a friend during those hard times.

Make up a melody to go with this song:

> Jesus, Jesus, when friends disappear
> Jesus, Jesus, You are always near.
> I am not alone—I'm Your very own;
> Jesus, Jesus, You are always near.

God sighting. Think about a time you were lonely. Did you talk to God about it? Did you listen for an idea, or did He send something or someone? Or did you forget Jesus was there entirely? To recognize God's presence, we usually need to converse with Him. Think about that. Paint a cross on your right thumbnail as a reminder.

Proceed with Care

✔ Make friend cookies by mixing up a batch of sugar cookie dough. Cut out two head shapes facing each other, noses touching. Bake. Write with icing your name and your friend's name on the faces. Wrap the cookie and give it to your friend.

✔ Make a "Happy Unbirthday" card for your friend. Mail it.

✔ Learn how to play Add-a-Line together so you can play it with a friend later on. Draw a grid of dots. The first player connects any two dots with a horizontal or vertical line. The second player may draw one line to connect any other two dots not already connected. The player who draws a line that closes a square may claim that square with his or her initial and take another turn. The winner has the most squares initialed. See illustration.

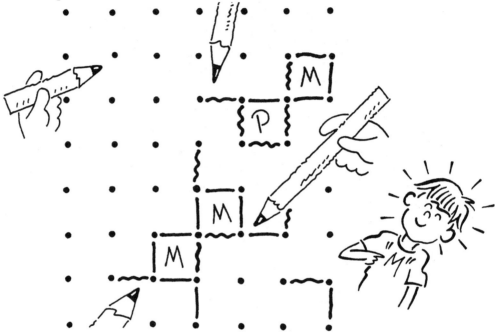

✔ There are many names for God, such as Shepherd and Elohim. Each name describes His love in a particular way. The name *Immanuel* means "God with us." We are never alone because Immanuel is with us. Where do you go when you feel lonely—a secret place? your bed? for a drive? Write "Immanuel" on an index card for each family member. Punch holes around it and lace it with a double strand of yarn: red for Jesus and your favorite color for you. Put the card in your lonesome spot.

✔ Friendship works both ways. Jesus likes for you to come to Him and stand by Him when others don't. Have you ever stuck up for Him? Have you ever had a tea for two and invited Him? Have you ever made Him a card? Do you ever apologize when you hurt His feelings? Do you tell Him, "I'm your friend"? Did you ever make Him a friendship bracelet? Think about what you might say or do as Jesus' friend.

Go in Peace

Write the word *FRIEND* vertically in capital letters. Then make an acrostic by starting a phrase with each letter on ways Jesus is our friend. For example F might be "faithful to me" and R might be "revs me up to take good risks." Use this as your prayer guide.

Because God First Loved Us, We Are Able to Love Others

Stop and Think

"You don't have to like everybody, but you can love everybody." Juan still struggled with this days after his Sunday school teacher said it. How could anybody love Eddie Clifton? Juan wondered.

Eddie Clifton's face, frozen into its perpetual sneer, surfaced in Juan's mind. Eddie had fat cheeks and lips and his chin just folded over his neck. Ugly jokes spewed out of his mouth, and he picked his nose. When he leaned against Juan's desk, his belly flopped over the papers. And he has bad breath, Juan added to the mental list.

I'm supposed to be Eddie Clifton's buddy? The idea seemed incomprehensible.

Eddie was absent Monday and Tuesday, but the class holiday couldn't go on forever. Even Mrs. Smith sighed when Eddie swaggered in the door Wednesday morning. He jammed his book bag into the cubby he shared with two other boys, smashing any hopes for unbroken chips in their lunch sacks. Then he added insult to injury by stuffing his coat in too. Eddie always wore a coat to school no matter what the temperature.

Moving toward his desk, Eddie managed to stomp on Elizabeth Dayton's new pencil, which she'd just dropped. He picked up both pieces and looked around laughing. "Uh, sorry." He flipped the pieces on her desk. "Keep your junk off the public freeway."

Apparently Elizabeth said something because the kids nearby laughed. Eddie looked back and glowered. He bumped Juan's elbow as he turned around. "Keep your elbows to yourself, Shrimp," he muttered, shoving Juan roughly.

Right. I can *love* Eddie Clifton, Juan thought.

After announcements, Mrs. Smith told the class to exchange math homework. Juan switched with Carl. The kids around Eddie must not have been switching with him today because when the teacher started reading answers, Eddie still had his own paper. Exasperated, Mrs. Smith asked Carl to switch. Juan swallowed his protest. He knew what Eddie would do to his math homework. The thing would bleed red marks and most or all of them would really be right. Juan sighed.

"And number 31 is 496," Mrs. Smith finished. Juan put a big 100% on Carl's paper and passed it back across the aisle. His own paper came back ripped on one edge and smudged. Sure enough, it looked like it had been through a battle. A circled "minus 15" stabbed the top. "Carl, can I borrow yours back for a minute?" Carl handed the perfect paper back, and Juan did a

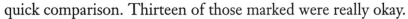

quick comparison. Thirteen of those marked were really okay.

Juan got up to show Mrs. Smith, but she waved him down. "We won't take grades today."

"Glad he got yours and not mine," Carl said. Juan didn't answer.

I think I've done pretty well, Juan thought. I didn't laugh at Eddie with Elizabeth. I didn't call him a name when he shoved me. I didn't blast him for wrecking my homework, and I kept quiet to Carl when I could have said something. I'll just totally block Eddie out of my mind. I won't do anything back to him.

While Juan was thinking this through, Mrs. Smith told the students to get partners. Everybody but Juan and Eddie had a partner. "Who doesn't have a partner?" the teacher asked.

Juan put up his hand. "Okay, you and Eddie get together then." Mrs Smith smiled at Juan.

Remember, Juan told himself as he scooted his desk next to Eddie's, I won't do anything back. And maybe I'll even say something nice.

Look and Listen

What if life were really fair? Then every time we did something to someone else, the same thing would happen to us. Think how that would be. Every time you helped someone, someone would help you. If you shared, another person would share with you. So far so good! When you lied, someone would lie to you. When you growled, you'd get growled at too. If you made someone late, someone would make you late. For every angry thought about someone, that person would think ill of you too. That's justice.

Imagine God doling out this kind of justice. It would be *exactly* fair. But we know that besides being just, God is also love. What if God ignored your bad tempers and selfish actions? Suppose when you took His name in vain, He did nothing. Suppose He just totally blocked you out of His life? It seemed pretty generous of Juan to do this toward Eddie, didn't it? Not hurting back takes a lot of effort.

Recite John 3:16 or read it together. Did you catch the part where God loves us so much that He blocks us out when we're unkind or thoughtless? It doesn't say that, does it? What does it say? (He gave His Son.) Oh, He *gave something*. He gave His *only* Son? But that must have been only for the good people of the world. What does Romans 5:8 say?

God defines love as giving everything to help someone— even someone mean—so that this person can be saved. This is even more than turning the other cheek like Juan was already doing; it also means going the extra mile. Jesus explains this in Matthew 5:39–48.

God sighting. How hard is it to love someone the way Jesus wants us to—especially someone who is a thorn in your side? It would be impossible if Jesus were not living in your heart! But since He does live there, He can help you. Does this mean letting bullies walk all over you? No. Jesus didn't let the Pharisees walk all over Him, but He still showed them love. Some of those bullies' lives were turned around because of Him! Think about who makes your life harder. Ask God to first show you how much God loves that person. Then ask Him to teach you to love the way Jesus does. Continue praying for this person daily all this week—not asking God to "fix him or her," but to show you what He sees.

✔ Make crabs together following these illustrations. A crab pinches when it's frightened. People often do too. What words might make a crabby person feel better? (You sound tired. Rough day?)

Proceed with Care

1. Fold paper plate in half.

2. Sketch dotted lines as shown.
Cut along dotted lines.

3. Open plate and turn over. Stick front tab through back slot.

4. Turn plate over. Push down on "body" to flatten slightly.

5. Bend bottom half of pinchers back a little. Fold back legs down.

141

- Make finger paint together. Soften one envelope of gelatin in ¼ cup cold water for five minutes. Set aside. In a heavy saucepan mix ½ cup cornstarch and 3 tablespoons sugar. Add 2 cups cold water gradually. Heat this mixture over medium heat until it thickens. Then add the gelatin and water. Divide the paint into sealable zipper bags and add food coloring and a squirt of dish soap per bag. Cool. Place newspapers under a cookie sheet and then spread the paint on the sheet's shiny surface. Use your finger to draw something wrong that you've done. Then wipe it off like God does when we ask Him to forgive us. Now draw something wrong that someone's done to you. Because you know how God wipes off your wrongs, you can wipe off other people's wrongs to you.

- Before family time, write each word of 1 John 4:19 on a separate index card. Place the cards in sight all over the house. During family time, tell the kids how many cards are in the house. Let them find them. Challenge the kids to put the cards in the correct order.

- Peter once asked Jesus if seven times was enough to forgive someone. Jesus answered that it should be 70 × 7. Count out this amount using pieces of cereal or M&M's candy.

- "A gentle answer turns away wrath but a harsh word stirs up anger" (Proverbs 15:1). Drop one drop of food coloring into a bottle of baby oil. Drop one drop of food coloring into a clear cup of just-boiled water. How does the visual help illustrate the proverb? Where does a gentle spirit come from? See Galatians 5:23.

John said, "Beloved, let us love one another" (1 John 4:7 KJV). Do you know how deeply God loves you? If not, ask Him to help you know His love for you. If you do know it, ask Him to fill up your soul with His love so much that your cup overflows to others. As you say either petition, fill a cup with water to overflowing as a visual symbol of your prayer.

Jesus, the Vine, Produces the Fruits of the Spirit in Us

Stop and Think

"Tony, you're a good helper today!" Mrs. Cann said. Tony beamed. His pudgy little fingers still had dirt under the fingernails, but he felt the genuine thrill of a true gardener. Nine little clay pots lined the kitchen window, each packed with rich brown dirt and a single African violet leaf.

Mrs. Cann folded the newspaper over the dead center stalk of the original plant, crumbling some of the dried yellow leaves they'd discarded. "Now's the perfect time to read a Frog and Toad book," she said, getting the well-worn copy of *Frog and Toad Together* off the shelf. She read aloud how Toad planted flower seeds and loudly commanded them to grow. Frog corrected Toad with wise advice. Toad became convinced that his seeds were now frightened, so he read them a story, sang songs to them, played music, and recited poems. Finally, they grew!

Little Tony closed the book with a satisfied sigh. He crossed his arms and was the picture of a proud farmer. He decided that singing to the violet leaves might encourage them to grow, so he and his mother sang "The Wheels on the

Bus," "Jesus Loves Me," and "Five Little Monkeys." That seemed good enough, and by then Tony was ready for something new.

Mrs. Cann helped Tony with his jacket zipper and waved to him as he peddled his bicycle around the backyard. Mrs. Cann smiled as she watched Tony's imaginative adventure. At the moment he was sword-fighting some bad guy behind his bike. At four, he could be trusted to stay within the boundaries of the yard, even though the property was large. He was headed for the orchard area when Mrs. Cann next glanced out the wide breakfast nook window.

Ten minutes later Tony came running inside, asking for the hand shovel. He's still thinking about gardening, Mrs. Cann surmised. "Remember not to dig near Daddy's fruit trees," she reminded.

"I won't," Tony called as he raced back outside. The next time Mrs. Cann looked out, Tony had made several small mounds of dirt. Each one had a single stick poking up. At first Mrs. Cann grinned, but then she looked at one of the sticks more closely. "Oh no!" Mrs. Cann raced out the door but stopped when she saw a pile of broken branches. "Tony," she said sharply. "Why did you break branches off Daddy's new apple tree?"

Tony looked up from his labor very surprised. "Mommy, Daddy will be so happy. Now there will be eight trees instead of one, and I did it all myself!" He beamed that very same satisfied air. "And every one has a little green apple already started on it!"

Mrs. Cann walked over to the remaining central trunk of the original tree. Only two branches remained on the tree. That was only because Tony couldn't reach them. Mrs. Cann stared at the ruined little tree then sat down. "Come and sit by me, Tony," she said.

Look and Listen

Read John 15:4–8. Grape vines work like apple trees. When you break off a branch, any maturing fruit on it is ruined. Each branch must stay connected to the main vine or trunk to get the nourishment required for the fruit. Jesus says, "I am the vine. You are the branches." He didn't say, "Now I'm going to make you all vines so you can each do what I've done." How did He say we would bear fruit like His (verse 5)? So how does a person "remain in Jesus"? Whatever we do to stay close and connected to Jesus is "remaining" in Him. What happens to grapes or apples that stay connected to the vine? They grow big and sweet. Jesus says that when you and I stay connected to Him the fruit He grows will last (verse 16).

So what is this fruit? Read verses 9–12. The fruit is love. From 1 Corinthians 13 we learn how Jesus loves His church. This passage is a model for how we can love one another. The Bible gives us a perfect definition of love.

Maybe your love fruits aren't fully ripe because you aren't kind all the time or ready to do God's business every day like Jesus did. But Jesus said that if you and I remain connected to Him, He will keep on maturing the love fruit started in us.

God sighting. When the word *connected* comes up this week in conversation or print, let it remind you that Jesus is our vine, our source of real strength and life. Pay attention for the word!

Proceed with Care

✔ Turn an apple upside down. On most, you can still see the tiny stamens of the apple blossom when God began this apple. Take a trip to an orchard, vineyard, or pumpkin patch and look for the fruits' various stages.

- ✔ Practice kind words together by working to complete a list of "Ten Reasons I'm Glad God Put You in Our Family."

- ✔ Stay connected by playing a game of hopscotch. Start by throwing a rock on square 1, then jump to it with both feet, turn, and jump back out. On your next turn, throw the rock to 2 and again jump on 1 and 2, then turn on 2, jump on 1, and jump out. Throw the rock on 3 and this time jump on 1 and straddle 2 and 3. Turn and jump with both feet on 1 and jump out. Continue. (See the illustration.)

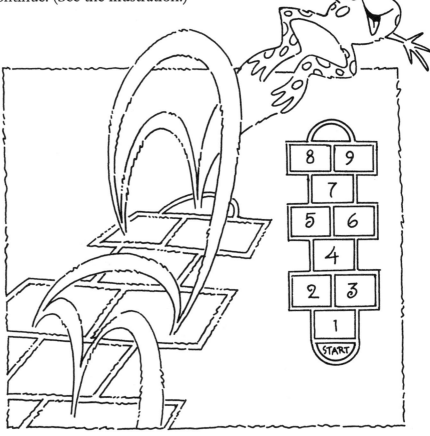

- Create your own Clue board game using the rooms in your house as the layout. Name the playing pieces after each other using an adjective starting with the same letter (Brilliant Bill or Courageous Connie). The mystery to solve is who sent a love message, where, and with what (singing telegram, roses, valentine, surprise gift, or poem).

- Make fruit sherbet: Heat 2 cups milk, 1 cup sugar, and a dash of salt until dissolved. Cool. Pour into a rectangular cake pan and freeze until solid. Mix 2 tablespoons lemon juice, 1½ cups any other juice (orange, lime, pineapple, strawberry), and 1 mashed banana (or ½ cup of any other mashed fruit). Then mix with the frozen milk mixture until slushy. Refreeze.

Go in Peace

Substitute your names in the appropriate places in John 15:5 where Jesus says, "I am the vine, *Tony* is the branch. If *Tony* remains in Me and I in *Tony*, *he* will bear much fruit." Use this as your prayer starter.

God Keeps His Promises

Stop and Think

"Where is he, your precious king of beasts?" hissed the salamander. "Don't waste your breath telling the others he will come like he said. The jackals control the forest now."

The deer struck his hoof near the salamander, and it fled away. He turned his large brown eyes back to his doe struggling to give birth. "There are so few of us left. This new life is indeed precious beyond measure." He shifted his flank to block a view of his emerging son from any vultures flying over-head in the west. A ray of sunlight fell on scars created when he had been caught by a band of marauding jackals. He had escaped, but his brother had not.

Looking into the dying sun, the deer thought about his father. A magnificent buck, his father had led the remnant of the deer population into these woods years ago to escape the jackal destruction of the wildlands. But finally, the jackals had migrat-ed here too. The last time the buck saw his father, his father had said, "Remember the king. He will come as he said with his mane flashing light and his claws bared. His teeth will crush our foes, and his might will break their hold on all the creatures of the forest. Look for him. He will come at the darkest hour."

The sun lay low like a streaming red river. "So many have died. How much longer can we last?" He turned his head to look at the newborn fawn. His doe was licking the baby deer clean and marking him as their own dear one. Your life will be hard, thought the buck. But perhaps you will see the king in your time.

Both adults flicked their ears forward at the sound of bay-ing in the distance. Immediately both thought of the little fawn. The birthing place was somewhat hidden in underbrush, but the mother instinctively nudged the fawn toward deeper cover. The buck crowded nearer as the baying sounded again. Then both waited fully alert with muscles taut, ready to spring.

Again the baying sounded, and this time closer. The pack was headed this way! The buck took one steady look back at the deer and fawn. "Courage," he urged. Then he bounded off to lead the jackals away.

The doe listened intently. After several minutes she heard the buck cry and the answering chorus of the jackals. "Let him run strong and swift!" the doe entreated.

The jackals dodged and snapped endlessly after the buck, seeming to come from every side. His breathing became labored and his eyes more strained. Slowly but surely they were surrounding him. The jackals laughed, their slavering jaws dripping threats. The buck finally set his rump toward a stand of trees and lowered his horns. "Some of you will die with me this day," he bugled.

The answering snarl of the jackal pack was cut short by a terrible roar from the right. Again and again the challenge bellowed. All eyes turned. There, racing with his massive haunches stretched out so that he practically flew, came an enormous, fierce lion!

Look and Listen

When we think about the promises God has made to us, we often think of a rainbow. Every rainbow reminds us that God said He'd never flood the entire earth again, no matter how evil things get. He has kept this promise.

We remember God's promise to make Abraham's descendants as many as the stars in the sky. The whole nation of Israel today, as well as the Jewish people scattered over the world, come originally from Abraham.

We remember that God told King David that the Messiah would be his descendant, and God kept that promise. Jesus was even born in David's birthplace.

God said Jesus would die for all the wrongs we've done and then come alive again after three days. The Bible records eyewitnesses to His death and resurrection.

Jesus promised to give the Holy Spirit to His followers, and He did just that on Pentecost!

God gives us, the people of His kingdom, the promise that Jesus will return. Read Matthew 24:4–14. What are some of the signs of these end times? What are we who are saved called to do (verse 13)?

God has kept His promises before. He will keep this one

too. We learn to trust all God's promises by watching Him keep His word. Which of God's promises to you have you seen? Has He been your sure foundation when everything was shifting (Isaiah 33:6)? Has God made your path straighten out in front of you when you couldn't see a way out of trouble (Proverbs 3:5–6)? Has He made you want to do His will when you were tempted to do wrong (Ezekiel 36:26–27)? Has God given you confident rest at times (Deuteronomy 33:12)?

God sighting. Watch for a rainbow this week. It may come in the sky or on the sheen of a puddle of oil. A piece of a rainbow may shine on the wall opposite a window or on the floor below a piece of crystal. Let the rainbow remind you of God's promises.

Proceed with Care

- ✔ Make a Promise File Box. Put Bible references on paper hearts and then look one up every day. Here are several: Romans 8:15; Isaiah 40:29; Isaiah 43:1; Isaiah 51:11; Isaiah 2:3; Isaiah 41:10; Isaiah 48:17; Psalm 23:4; Psalm 114:11; 1 John 1:9; 2 Peter 1:2; Jude 24; Ephesians 1:13.

- ✔ Sharpen those "memory muscles." Lay 10 to 15 objects in a line. Have your family look at the objects for one minute. Then have them go into a different room and try to write or draw as many as they can recall. You can play this memory game with partners too. How many could each person recall?

- ✔ Try the verbal memory game. One person starts by saying, "On Noah's ark were two fleas." The next person adds, "On Noah's ark were two fleas and two zebras." Continue until no one can remember the whole string of animals. (Make this game easier for young children by

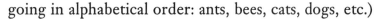

going in alphabetical order: ants, bees, cats, dogs, etc.)

✔ Dampen paper and lay it on newspaper. Then draw a rainbow with colored chalk. The color will blur slightly.

✔ Outline a rainbow on waxed paper. Paint it with liquid starch. Then arrange small bits of tissue paper to make the colored bands. Let it dry. Peel off the waxed paper.

✔ Make a Promises Bag for your pastor to give to someone he visits. Decorate a paper bag. Write John 3:16 on a craft-stick cross and put it in the bag. Drop in a small compass tagged: "Jesus said—I am the way" (John 14:6). Include two napkins marked: "Do not worry about what to eat. Your heavenly Father knows what you need" (Luke 12:22–31, paraphrase). Trace one hand, fingers together, on folded tagboard. Cut so that you have two matching hands. Glue one hand onto one edge of a spring clothespin and the other hand on the other edge. Now the hands will open when you squeeze. Write "Ask, Seek, Knock" on one hand. Put three or four index cards into the hands which have printed prayers suggested by your family. Finally, add any other marked objects from the promise references included in this family time.

✔ Add to a picture of Jesus that you have in your house a ribbon banner that reads: Coming Soon!

✔ One of God's precious promises is that nothing—not life, not death, not circumstance—can separate us from His love. People cross their fingers when they say they will do something that they do not intend to really do. When you cross your fingers, let it stand instead for the promise that God is always as close as our two fingers.

Place a doll in a wooden bowl or basket. Prop it up on four pillars. The doll represents a person cradled in trust. Trust is held up by four pillars: truthfulness, promise keeping, willing service, and steadfast love. Any time one of these pillars gets knocked down, like when someone lies, breaks a promise, doesn't help, or leaves us in the lurch, trust can topple. God always keeps these pillars strong because trust is important to Him. Use the trust basket to help you praise Him.

Pray together: God, You always tell the truth so we trust what You say in Your Word. Please help us to be truthful, keep our promises, be willing servants, and to show our love for others through You. You gave up Your perfect Son for our sins; He is the ideal of trust and forgiveness. Amen.

Go in Peace

Special Times
Special Times
Special Times
Special Times
Special Times
Special Times
Special Times

God Takes Time to Love Us

Stop and Think

"Whatcha doing, Poppi?" Kristil asked her great-grandpa. She stepped gingerly around the half-completed rocking horse Poppi was making for her little sister. Sawdust stuck to the bottom of her shoes but she didn't care. She liked the grainy smell of wood out here, and she loved her Poppi.

Mr. Wendler looked up from the battered desk where he was working and chuckled. "I might have known you'd hunt me down. Can't keep anything secret from you." Kristil bent down to look at the rocking horse. "Don't you be telling your sister about that now."

"I won't," she answered, running her hand over the wooden curve of its head.

"Hmm," Poppi said. "Lucky for me you're good at keeping surprises." He turned back to the desk.

"What is that you're writing on?" Kristil asked, pointing to the shiny paper.

"It's this year's calendar. Here, you can help me." Poppi pulled a stool over, and Kristil climbed up. "Put one of these gold stars on the number I tell you." He looked in a dusty brown leather book and said, "Thirteen."

Kristil licked the star and stuck it next to the 13 on the calendar. Then Poppi wrote "Dana's birthday" in the square. He flipped a page on the calendar. "Now put a star on 17."

Kristil picked another star out of the little red box and put it next to the 17. Poppi wrote "Barbara's birthday."

Kristil's eyes opened wide. "Oh, these are birthdays! You're putting all my cousins' birthdays on your new calendar. Is mine in your brown book?"

"Of course, it is. Do I ever forget your birthday?" Poppi pointed at May, and Kristil saw her name printed by the 14. She remembered the dollhouse Poppi gave her last year for her fifth birthday. She leaned her elbows on the desk.

"I love birthdays!" she mused. "I love the presents."

"It would still be a birthday even without presents," Poppi answered. "Back when I was your age the Depression was happening, so there were no presents like the ones you get."

"What's 'depression'?" Kristil asked.

"When I was a little boy, our country had some money problems. Most dads didn't have money for anything besides food. Lots of families had almost no money at all, so they planted vegetables and mended the clothes they had so as not to need new ones. Birthdays still got celebrated but without store-bought presents. We didn't get more than an orange or an apple and maybe a candy stick for Christmas either."

Kristil was aghast. "How can you say you celebrated when you didn't get anything?"

"I didn't say I didn't get anything. You can give someone love without buying something. For instance, you know what your mother likes a whole lot more than presents? She likes someone to lend a hand with chores around the house."

"Is that why you always wash the dishes when you come over?" Kristil asked.

"Yep, that's why. But you know, your Aunt Cella now, she'd rather just take a walk together—just walk and talk. That's what she likes."

"What do I like, Poppi?" Kristil asked.

"Don't you know? You like to hear me tell you how terrific you are! You've always liked to be told that you're good at keeping secrets or finding things or singing." Poppi ran his hand over her hair. "And I love these blonde curls of yours too."

Kristil's eyes twinkled, and she reached over to hug her Poppi. "Oh, that's what I like best," Poppi said. "I'll take these big hugs any day." He gave Kristil an extra squeeze.

Look and Listen

Did you know God keeps track of every living thing every moment? He knows about each blade of grass. He knows if a sparrow falls from its nest. He knows about every baby before he or she is born. He tells the wind what to do. That keeps Him pretty busy, don't you think? But God still makes time to love us. Look up Genesis 1 in your Bible. Name some of the things God was busy doing. Now read Genesis 2:1–3.

God set apart one day every week to make time to be close to us and remind us that life isn't just about working. He knew that sometimes we get so busy with life that we might overlook being thoughtful to those we love. So God said that there should be a special day for loving. For many people that day is Sunday. For others, like pilots and ambulance drivers, that day has to be a different day. Still, we can care about showing love to God and to each other by making a regular time on the calendar.

I wonder how God is planning to love you this year? Will He put it in your grandpa's mind to get a gift God knows you'd like for your birthday? Will He send you a friend to hug you on a day when He'd like to hug you? Will He remind you of how much He loves you when you're telling Him you feel lonesome? Will He send someone to help you with a big chore? Will He nudge your teacher to say something nice about some schoolwork you really tried hard to do well?

God sighting. Do you remember a time God was loving you this past year?

Proceed with Care

✔ Take out a new calendar and put stickers on family members' and loved ones' birthdays. Schedule a few special Children's Choice days for bowling, horseback riding, hiking, or whatever each child likes. Consider Daddy dates or Mommy dates too for one-on-one time.

✔ Praising children for accomplishments is one way of showing love. Use waterproof fabric to make a "We're proud" flag (or make a paper one and seal it with clear adhesive paper). Staple it to a pole and fly it anytime someone in the family does something praiseworthy.

✔ Spend some time on New Year's Day making an audio- or videotape. Reflect on noteworthy events, such as: "I lost my two front teeth," "I can say all the times tables," or "I started playing soccer, and I had nine assists and six goals." Report on vacation or holiday highlights too. (I like to record favorite gifts the children received so that someday, as a grandma, I'll know what to get the grandchildren.)

✔ Match food with certain holidays. Make each festival unique. Have an open house with a bottomless pot of chili and fresh bread for all who come. Guests can bring desserts to share.

✔ Take time to brainstorm simple activities for the family to do together. Save the list so you're sure to include them this year.

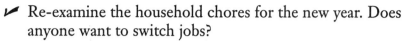

- Re-examine the household chores for the new year. Does anyone want to switch jobs?

- Start a family New Year's Eve party tradition. Each child may invite one or two friends and their families over for an evening of table games. Set up six to eight games depending on the number of guests. Fun games include old-fashioned ones, such as Spoons, Cooties, and Racko as well as newer games that can be played in a short period of time. Set a timer for 10 minutes per game session and have everyone play with different people every time. Give the winner of each session two points and the second-place winner one point. The grand prize winner gets first pick at the gift-wrapped white elephants each guest brought to the party. Put on party hats and serve New Year's Eve snacks.

Go in Peace

What did you learn this time about God and about ourselves? Write down the words or say them aloud. Now turn the words into a prayer thanking God for taking the time to love us and remember everything about us.

Epiphany: Jesus Is Our King

Stop and Think

Prince Elson worked hard to match his father's long stride as they passed through the arched side hall. King Elohim did everything in a determined way, even walking. The stone floors rang with the steady sound of his steps, reassuring the servants in earshot that all was well and safe in the kingdom.

One old servant crossed behind the pair and paused to smile at the upturned face of the prince, so serious, so intent.

"Father, this new strategy of Luce's; I do not understand it. How can he hope that our people would be so foolish as to each try to be king? Who would believe that we can all live together if we do as Luce says? If each takes care only of himself, how is that being a true king?"

King Elohim stopped by an opening in the white stone wall. He looked out over the vastness of his realm, laid out below like a tapestry. "How indeed," he answered. "Who can be unselfish enough to work for the good of all over whatever appears to be good for one? Who can ponder all the decisions that affect so many, one woven into another? Who will sacrifice himself to take the first onslaught from Luce and his evil armies like a true king? Who will spend night after night with the sick and dying, the love for them outstripping the desire for his own rest? Who is wise enough to know when to intervene and when to allow this one or that to learn the consequences of their wrong ways? Who can give them what they need when they clamor only for what they wish?"

Prince Elson left his father's questions unanswered for a full minute. Then he gazed out over the land and spoke into the air, "They would be like sheep without a shepherd, Father."

King Elohim looked down at his young son tenderly. He put his hands on Elson's shoulders. Then with the incredible calmness that always surrounded the king, he said, "That is why, Son, you must go and live among them. In due time, Luce will have convinced great numbers of them that you and I don't even exist. Some will play at being kings in order to feel power over others. The weak ones will suffer—those with no one to protect them. When the time is right, you will go to stand against Luce and his armies."

Prince Elson's eyes were steady as he faced his father. "I

love them too, Father. You and I are one in wanting to save them. I will do whatever you tell me. While I am down there, I know you can see all of the kingdom from up here. I will go wherever you tell me and do as you direct me." He paused a moment and then grasped his father's outstretched arms. "And we will win, Father!"

"Yes, my son. *We will win!*" Fire was in their eyes, the fiery spirit of victory.

Look and Listen

Read Matthew 2:1–12. What were the three presents given to Jesus when He was born? Did you get any of those when you were born? Maybe you got a gold bracelet, but more likely you got clothes, a stroller, and some rattles. Why do you think men who lived so far away would bring presents like these to Jesus—who did they think had just been born (verse 2)?

Gold seems like a logical gift to give a king, but incense was mostly used by priests when worshiping God (Exodus 30:34–38). Myrrh was a spice used in the wrappings of people who had died.

I wonder if those Wise Men understood that someone incredible had just come into the world? They gave Him gifts for a king, for a priest, and for a dying Savior. Look at the next time in Jesus' life when He was given myrrh—John 19:39. When was that?

How is Prince Elson like Jesus?

Epiphany, January 6th, is the day Christians remember that God is Elohim, the Mighty Creator and King of the universe. Like the Magi, we worship Jesus too. He is the One who loves us enough to be our King; He puts our needs before His own. That's why He came to this earth—to keep us from the lies and death that Satan likes. If you were a Magi, what would you have given the baby King?

God sighting. Memorize John 3:16: "For God so loved the world that He gave His one and only Son that whoever believes in Him shall not perish but have eternal life." Then see if you can find someone else who can recite it to you. (You might ask a grandparent, a Christian friend, or your pastor.)

Proceed with Care

✔ Make crowns by folding and cutting paper as illustrated. Leave 1½ inches on the bottom for the rim. Open it up, turn it inside out, and tape the two left rim sides together and the two right rim sides together for a continuous circle. The crown will be a bit floppy but fun, and it's so easy to make!

1. FOLD!

2. CUT!

1½"

3. OPEN UP!

4. TURN OVER!

5. TAPE ENDS!

6. TAPE TOGETHER TO FORM A CIRCLE!

162

✔ Candied fruit peel or gumdrops are traditional sweets for Epiphany because of their jeweled appearance. Think of jewels in a king's crown. Decorate a cake with candy "jewels" by cutting a square cake into triangular fourths. Line up the triangles with the points facing up, ice with yellow icing, and add candy jewels.

✔ Paint each other's feet using finger paints. (Thin any regular tempera paint with dish soap—it comes off easier too.) Then one at a time, walk across a length of white paper, all in the same direction. You can use the white side of wrapping paper if you don't have a roll of white paper. Wash one another's feet. Draw a star at the top of the paper, then title your witness banner: "We follow the star to Jesus!"

✔ Epiphany is also called Twelfth Night because it is the final day of the Christmas season. Remember the song "The 12 Days of Christmas"? Draw each of the 12 scenes and sing the song by popping up on the parts you drew. Next year leave the crèche up all 12 days with the Wise Men figures getting closer each day. On Epiphany set them near baby Jesus. Save a final Christmas gift for each child to open.

✔ Some families serve wassail on Epiphany. Make wassail by simmering the following for 20 minutes: 2 quarts apple cider, ½ cup brown sugar, 3 ounces each of frozen lemon and orange juice concentrate, 3 cloves, 3 allspice, 1 teaspoon nutmeg, and 1 teaspoon cinnamon.

✔ Make today the day your family writes thank-you notes for Christmas gifts. Reprint some of the snapshots of your children opening gifts to enclose with the letters. Use the gift wrap from the sender to make the card!

Pray this traditional prayer from Saint Columba:

> Alone with none but Thee, my God
> I journey on my way.
> What need I fear, when Thou art near
> O King of night and day?
> More safe am I within Thy hand
> Than if a host did round me stand.

Go in Peace

Valentine's Day: God Desires a Love Relationship with Each of Us

Bump went the staff against Missy's side.

Bump. Bump. Missy turned back toward the rest of the flock that had already gone ahead. But after a few yards, she again turned off the path. Once again—*bump*. Still looking left, Missy bleated.

"Missy, Missy," the shepherd sighed. "Always wanting to go your own way. You can't see the poison berries over on that other side. You'd think their pretty color makes them good to eat. Better to go the way I lead and stay away from trouble." The shepherd tapped Missy's left side again to move her toward the right. She finally moved on.

Later when they were at the pasture, the shepherd rubbed Missy's face. "That's good, Missy. See how nice this is? Look down at that good green grass. Trust me, Missy. I care about keeping you healthy and safe." Missy lowered her head and began to munch. She was content—for the

Stop and Think

moment, at least.

Two weeks later the shepherd began herding his flock through the narrow mountain pass to the green tableland he'd prepared. The sheep had to go single file through one section. Missy decided to be difficult and balked several times. The shepherd gently urged her on. "It's okay, Missy. I'm here. I won't let you fall." He watched her closely and when she began stepping off to the left, he caught the curved end of his crook around her left front leg to pull her back onto the path.

The shepherd managed to get all the sheep up to the tableland where he kept a watchful eye out for lions and bears. It was also the time of year he carefully inspected each sheep and lamb and put salve on any sores. Missy had several because she'd often wandered into rocks and thornbushes. As the shepherd anointed her, he said, "Well, my little Missy, you sure are a stubborn one. You take more watching than all the other 99 put together!" Missy bleated.

"I love you though, Missy, because you are my little lamb. Now I'm going to do something you won't like. I'm going to hobble your back legs. Then you'll not go off so easily. Whenever we move to another place, I will carry you here inside my tunic. You'll get used to my smell and my voice. Hopefully, Missy, you'll learn to trust me and stay close to me."

After the shepherd put the hobbles on Missy, he scooped up a cup brimming with clear, cold water. Missy drank, lapping water every which way and getting the shepherd wet. He just laughed. Then he picked her up, tucked her inside his coat next to his heart, and began calling the others by name to follow him.

Jesus told a story about a father and his two sons. One son started out hard to love but became easy to love. The other son started easy to love but became hard to love. Still the father patiently loved each one. Read both stories in Luke 15:11–32.

How do you think the younger son felt when he realized that his father was already out watching for him? What do you think he believed about his father after receiving sandals, a ring, a robe, and then hearing his dad say, "Let's have a feast and celebrate for this son of mine ... was lost and is found!"?

How do you think the older son felt seeing his father come out of the party to talk to him? What words did this son hear that let him know his father loved him very deeply (verse 31)? Would you find it hard to love someone who was criticizing you? How does someone love in that situation?

How are Missy and the older son different? (One ran away and the other didn't.) How are they alike? (Both balked at the shepherd/father's desire for a love relationship.) How is God like the shepherd and the father?

God sighting. Are you ever hard to love? Talk about times you can remember being difficult to love. Do you think God loved you even then? (Yes! God's desire is that you'll stay close forever!)

**Proceed
with Care**

✔ Make pizza dough into a heart shape. Spoon on the pizza sauce and add shredded mozzarella cheese. Serve with cherry 7-Up soda pop.

✔ Decorate a can and title it "Love Notes." Set slips of paper and pencils nearby. Make a note of any time a family member demonstrates love: helping, listening, giving a gift, hugging, saying something nice. Put each note in the can. Open the can and read the notes during your next family time.

✔ Decide on a phrase you'd like to say more during the rest of February, such as: "My day is better because you're here"; "I knew you could do it"; "You're my favorite grown-up!" or "This can wait; you're important too."

✔ Together, cut out paper hearts. Have everyone go into a different room and write messages on them. Tape the hearts on doorjambs all over the house and then have everyone come sit in the kitchen. Let everybody finish the sentence "Love is _____." After that, dash around the house to read the notes.

✔ Come up with new ways to send a valentine. Write "You slipped into my heart" on a banana; "I go for you" on the bottom of your shoes; or put a thumbprint on a card over the words "Thumbody loves you."

✔ Send a secret love message. Completely wet a sheet of typing paper. Lay it on a flat surface. Lay another wetted paper over it. Write your message on the top sheet using a ballpoint pen and pressing firmly. Carefully lift off the top sheet and discard. Allow the bottom paper to dry thoroughly. The message will disappear, only to be visible again when that paper is wet.

✔ Cut several heart shapes from sponges. Use a spring clothespin for a handle and press each onto an ink pad or a shallow dish of paint. Print hearts on several sheets of paper. When the heart prints are dry, write a message of love to God on each one and tape them on the windows.

✔ Put a note on the ceiling above your child's bed which reads: "I love you. Signed, God."

↙ Before family night, cut out the letters for love as illustrated. Mix them up and give a few pieces to each person without saying what word these pieces spell. See if your family can come up with the letters and then the word. Discuss how your family "spells" love in other ways, such as waiting for one another or holding the door.

↙ Roll up your child in a blanket and carry him or her all over, finally tossing the child onto a bed or sofa. Without moving or peeking, can he or she guess which room you're in? "Losers" get tickled.

↙ Play a game of I Love. Cut a heart out of cardboard and write "I love" on the top. Draw an arrow pointing down to the bottom of the heart. Clear the table and let the first player stand on a chair and drop the heart. Whomever the heart points toward most nearly gets a hug from the player and a spoken "I love you." Take turns.

✔ Cut two large hearts out of paper. Glue the sides together but leave the top open. Add a loop for a handle. Write Bible passages on cards, such as John 13:34; Romans 8:28; John 1:23; John 13:35; Romans 8:39; and John 15:12. Place these inside the holder and give them to your grandma and grandpa.

Go in Peace

Read these words of God but substitute your name in appropriate places: "This is what the LORD says ... 'Fear not, for I have redeemed *Missy*; I have summoned *Missy* by name; *she* is Mine. ... *Missy* [is] precious and honored in My sight ... I love *Missy*'" (Isaiah 43:1–4).

Ash Wednesday:
God Confronts Our Sin, Invites Confession, and Forgives

Stop and Think

Peter quickly opened all the windows in his bedroom, even though it was February. He waved his arms around trying to get the smoke out of the room. The burned part of his pajama bottoms made the room smell, so he slipped out and moved quietly towards the back door. "Please God, don't let Mom or Dad wake up." He slowly turned the knob and carefully opened the door. "Click!" The door sounded loud in the stillness of early morning. Peter stopped like a trapped rabbit. But no one came. Once more he moved toward the big garbage can outside. He crammed the pajamas to the bottom.

The snow on his bare feet felt like needles, so he dashed inside, shivering as he passed through the kitchen. Back in his room he breathed a sigh and then began sniffing. Would they smell it? he wondered. He glanced down at the throw rug that now covered a burned spot on the carpet. Everything appeared normal. He decided to act natural and turn on Saturday morning cartoons. Peter traipsed off into the living room feeling very clever.

Half an hour later Dad passed through the living room on his way to the kitchen. "Mornin', Sport," he said. "Sleep okay?"

Peter's stomach flip-flopped but he managed a bright smile. "Sure, Dad." He could hear Dad making coffee. He liked to serve Mom a cup in bed on Saturdays. A little later he passed through again holding two cups. Peter glanced up nervously.

Then Dad came back in the living room. "Son, you want to tell me why your bedroom windows are wide open?"

"Ah, gosh." Peter said. Drat! I forgot the windows. What can I say? he thought. "I think I've got a fever or something because I started feeling really hot," Peter said.

"You don't look sick," Dad answered, watching him.

"Oh, I'm fine now," Peter said.

"Let's get those windows shut, shall we?" Peter jumped up, and Dad followed him into the bedroom. Dad began pulling out the desk chair to sit down. "So let's try this again. Tell me about the windows."

Peter nervously said, "Let me close this other one, Dad."

When he turned around, Dad was pushing the throw rug out of the way so he could get the chair turned around. They both stared at the exposed black spot on the rug.

"What's this?" Dad asked.

Choose your own ending:

1. "Oh, I spilled a little black paint there when I was working on my model. Mom said to just cover it with the rug until we clean the carpets."

Dad leaned down to look closely. "This isn't paint, Peter. It's burned."

Peter didn't know what to say. Dad waited, but still Peter said nothing. Dad looked at the windows and then at Peter's mismatched pajamas. "You're lying. You know how I feel about lying." His voice had become stern and hard.

Still Peter said nothing, but his ears burned hot. He knew he was in for it. What's so wrong? he thought. It's not as bad as he's making it to be. Both tempers rose and hard feelings between Peter and his dad grew.

2. "Gee, I don't know, Dad. It's the first time I've seen it. I bet somebody else was in here—maybe when Uncle Doug was here with Andrew. I bet that was it."

"Well, Andrew should have told us and not tried to hide it."

Dad was still poking at the spot when Peter let his shoulders relax. Fooled him, Peter smirked silently.

3. After some hesitation Peter confessed, "I was fooling around with matches and my pajama pants caught on fire, so I had to take them off. Then I banged them with my shoe to put the fire out, but the carpet burned some."

"You know what your mother and I have always told you about fire."

"I know I disobeyed you, Dad. I'm really sorry."

"You also tried to deceive us." Dad looked deeply disappointed.

Peter realized he'd not only disobeyed but tried to lie too. Lying was a sin. Peter stood still, looking at his dad. Then he walked over to him and said, "Dad, I will pay for the pajamas and whatever the rug costs from my allowance. Lies can't be paid back except to say I will never do it again. Whatever punishment you think is right, I'll do."

Dad nodded and then said, "Let me think about that. For now, I'm glad you are sorry."

"I wish you'd forgive me, Dad. I don't want you to wonder the next time if I'm lying or not."

"It will be better when you show me that you can tell the truth even though you're afraid. I forgive you."

Look and Listen

Read about someone who disobeyed in Jonah 1, 3, and 4. What did Jonah do wrong to begin with? Jonah prayed to God inside the fish (chapter 2) asking God to help him. What did Jonah do the second time God told him to go to Nineveh (3:3)? Jonah got angry with God for forgiving Nineveh when the king and the people repented. He stomped over to a place on the east side of the city, still hoping God would destroy Nineveh. After awhile the sun beat down on Jonah. God caused a big vine to grow up and make some shade.

At dawn the next day, Jonah was still sitting out there, hoping to see fire and brimstone. Instead, God sent a worm to chew through that vine and sent a blistering hot wind. Jonah boiled! He was mad at God, mad at the heat, and mad that the vine died. Then God confronted Jonah:

"Do you have a right to be angry about the vine?"

"I do," he said. "I am angry enough to die."

But the LORD said, "You have been concerned about this vine, though you did not tend it or make it grow. It sprang up overnight and died overnight. But Nineveh has more than a hundred and twenty thousand people who cannot tell

their right hand from their left, and many cattle as well.
Should I not be concerned about that great city?"
(Jonah 4:9–11)

We don't know if Jonah ended up confessing his hatred or not. The account ends with God's question. Perhaps God left the ending open so we could be in Jonah's shoes and answer that last question.

What was missing between Dad and Peter in endings 1 and 2? (Forgiveness.) If Jonah confessed, surely he would have been forgiven for his anger and jealousy. God is very forgiving.

God sighting. Has God ever confronted you because you did something wrong or didn't do something you knew was right? Why does He do that? (See Psalm 66:18–19.)

Proceed with Care

✔ Cut out headlines from today's newspaper that show people who have sinned by breaking God's rules. Lay them in a big circle on the floor and stand in the center of it. Together read 1 John 1:8–10. Ask God for forgiveness.

✔ God's Law—the Ten Commandments—acts as a mirror so we can see that we are not perfect. Put clear cellophane over a mirror. Standing close to it, outline your facial features with indelible marker. Although we see our flaws clearly here, this face is much loved by God!

✔ Sit on a basketball. Extend your legs and cross your ankles. Now try to write your name on a pad of paper without falling. Some things, like confessing, are hard to do, but keep at it!

✔ Make a come-back can. Punch two holes in the bottom of a coffee can and two holes in the plastic lid. Cut a rubber band so it makes a single line instead of a loop. Poke it through all the holes, cross it as illustrated, and then tie it so that it is once again a continuous loop. Attach a weight like a rock with string to the center of the rubber band. When you roll the can away from you, it will come back. The words "I'm sorry" and "I forgive you" help people come back to us.

1 PUNCH TWO HOLES IN BOTTOM OF COFFEE CAN AND TWO HOLES IN LID.

2 CUT RUBBER BAND SO IT MAKES A SINGLE "LINE," PASS IT THROUGH ALL HOLES AND TIE KNOT OUTSIDE LID.

3 BE SURE TO CROSS THE RUBBER BAND.

4 ATTACH HEAVY WEIGHT (LIKE A ROCK) TO CENTER OF RUBBER BAND.

Who taught you how to forgive? Who do you think taught that person to forgive? How far back do you think this goes? Yes! God was the first to forgive, and He's still the best at it! Thank Him for teaching you how to forgive and giving you the Holy Spirit to prompt you to forgive even when it's hard.

Go in Peace

First Day of Spring: God Brings Joy

Stop and Think

She lay across her daughter's bed, still clutching the bedclothes. The late morning sun filtered through the upstairs window. The night had been so long, watching her daughter's chest rise and fall so faintly. The morning brought on another spate of coughing. She'd wiped the blood from her daughter's mouth, holding up her head. Three weeks of torture and fear made the mother's eyes heavy. She laid her head on the bed next to her daughter's weary form.

She looked at her daughter's pale cheeks. Dark circles made the girl's eyes smudges in her face. Oh, Joy, you have been light and laughter to me, the mother thought. I remember the morning you were born, and we named you Joy. Your father read your special verse from the Psalms. "Weeping may endure for a night, but joy cometh in the morning" (Psalm 30:5 KJV).

"We almost lost you then," the woman mused. "The pregnancy was difficult—we both nearly died in labor. But you came in the morning just like the psalm said. You brought such happiness with you. Oh, Joy, stay here with us." She prayed, "Lord God, spare her life!"

The coughing began again, racking the slender body. "Faith! Help me!" the mother called. A servant came running, and the two women held the 12-year-old's shoulders between them. Each cough seemed so impossibly severe, and the child drew breath with greater and greater difficulty.

"Hold on, Joy. The master must come soon with the rabbi," Faith whispered more to comfort the mother than the child.

But the little girl rasped with such a terrible scraping sound, and the time between breaths seemed an eternity. This last one seemed to deflate even more slowly, and the two women tensed.

Minutes passed. Time stopped.

Tears trickled down the old servant's cheeks. She began to lay the child back down. "Let me hold her," the mother choked. Faith left the room, the silence unbroken. Gray shadows numbed the mother's soul. "Oh, Jairus, we've lost her. This is no Joy; there will never be joy again." Hours passed as the mother held her daughter. She crooned and rocked, crooned and rocked. Downstairs the wailing women gathered to cry out the loud mourning of death. "This is a house of sorrow now," the mother said aloud. At last she lay her daughter down and stood bent over like an old, old woman. Then she made her way down the creaking stairs.

She didn't notice when the wailing stopped. She looked up when Jairus stood over her. "Now he comes—too late," she thought.

Four other men, strangers, stood with her husband. One seemed so confident, so strong. He looked at the mother with such compassion, even a hint of something—what was it? Perhaps it was eagerness, no—anticipation. They followed Him upstairs. He walked to the bed and reached for the girl's hand. Then He spoke, "Little girl, I say to you, get up."

Tears sprang anew to the mother's eyes as her daughter sat up. A sob broke from her throat. "Oh, Joy! Oh, Joy!" She leapt forward, dropped to her knees, and clasped the living child to her breast.

The man's eyes danced, and His great, warm mouth laughed as He said, "Feed her! She's hungry!"

176

Look and Listen

God knows that people who have had great sadness often can't see. So God helps us by putting signs of truth in our lives. The truth is that joy *can* come after weeping. We call one of God's signs "spring."

After a gray winter where trees seem dark and dead and birds seldom sing, God calls forward the liquid colors stored in impossibly small seeds. Thin green pencil points spring up like slow-motion rockets and then burst into fireworks of color. Who could have guessed that such life and joy could come from gray-brown days?

God is always causing spring's joy in the middle of gray emptiness. Can you remember a time when you felt sad and dreary—maybe when a friend moved, a pet or close family member died, or you experienced a sudden turnaround in a relationship? Talk about that time.

We tend to put ourselves into boxes, thinking that the walls we see are all there is. God knocks holes in our boxes with unexpected events. The Bible is full of stories where God caused unexpected joy—Naomi, Leah, David, Peter, Paul, and Dorcas to name a few. God is always reminding us that this life is the life *He gives*, and it is always different from the gray winter we expect.

God sighting. Spring is probably God's most obvious sign that He brings surprising joy. Look for other ways He shows us joy. Maybe you will see it in a cocoon, a tree stump that has sprouted, a snowfall that lays sparkling frosting over everything, or a rainbow at the end of a storm.

✔ Sometimes the first day of spring is overcast. That's the right day for a "Hosanna Banana" celebration. Wear bright yellow clothes, cut yellow pictures from magazines, use yellow napkins and yellow candles, and cover surfaces with as much yellow as you can! Serve yellow foods like macaroni and cheese, corn, acorn squash, sweet potatoes, corn chips, mangos, or pineapples. Make banana splits for dessert. Turn ordinary games into banana games like Pin-the-Banana-on-the-Tree or Fruit Bowl Upset whenever "banana switch" is called. Interview a banana or have a debate between a bunch of bananas and a bunch of grapes. Have a banana puppet show by drawing faces on the peels and dressing your bananas.

✔ Spring brings out the cleaning bug. Assign each person a cabinet, a drawer, and a shelf to clean for a "spotless seal of approval" treat.

✔ Make gingerbread houses. Ice four upright graham crackers to form the walls. Use two more for a peaked roof. Let the crackers dry and then ice them together. During family time let members use icing to glue on gumdrops, peppermints, coconut, and whatever candies you might have saved from last Halloween!

✔ The first day of spring is a scheduled fire drill at our house. Set off the alarm and see that everyone remembers where the designated meeting place is. Ask the older children for their plan of escape in case the regular route is blocked.

✔ Open a peanut by carefully slipping your thumbnail between the two halves. Examine the inside closely to find the tiny dry leaf and stem tucked into the bottom of the meat. Tuck some lima bean seeds into a wet paper towel. Slip this into a resealable plastic bag and check it after a few days. Again, carefully pry apart the seed so you can see the little growing plant zygote. This little plant is already green even though the seed is white and the water is clear! Take a trip to the hardware store and select a packet of flower or vegetable seeds for each child in your family. Start plants in pots on a sunny window ledge.

✔ Give the children seed catalogs and let them create a marvelous spring garden scene by cutting out the illustrations. Draw your house on paper and let the children designate garden areas.

Go in Peace

What did God bring to your mind or heart most during this family time? Talk about that. Then turn your conversation into a prayer to God thanking Him for the new life spring brings and for the new life He gave us through His Son!

Easter Day: Jesus Is Victorious over Death

Stop and Think

David felt rich. His new shirt crinkled as he turned to admire Mother's flowery dress and hat. His father wore a suit. David believed his parents were surely the most marvelous people in the whole church. He even had to admit that Alyssa's new dress made her face shine. She was swinging her legs just now on the other side of Mother. David knew Alyssa liked the way light danced on her new shiny white shoes.

The church looked as magnificent as David felt. He counted 55 Easter lilies, their white trumpets blaring. If that flower could talk, I bet it would be shouting, "Attention! Important event is about to happen!" Lilies definitely fit Easter, thought David.

From the flowers, David's eyes moved to the white satin draped over the altar. A lamb was stitched on the front. It was holding onto an empty cross. Then David stared up at the great cross above the altar. Today a bright butterfly was fastened on one side. Little paper butterflies hung all around the sanctuary. Alyssa and David had made several of them in Sunday school. The breeze made them flutter as if they were alive.

Just then, the brass trumpets began to play "Jesus Christ Is Risen Today." People stood up and David looked over to see his father and mother sharing a hymnal. The church choir came down the aisle. David recognized people from the Bible study group. Their robes made them look bigger than usual. The organist played louder, and people sang louder. David felt like shouting aloud.

The whole church service was magnificent. When everyone began leaving at the end, people smiled more, and pockets of laughter trilled around David. A woman handed Alyssa and David special baskets for the egg hunt. David quickly found a couple of friends. "Go for the gold ones," advised one friend. "You get bonuses for those."

While the parents looked on, the children scampered around finding the blue, yellow, green, and red eggs. David found six eggs, and one was gold! He ran over to his mother but stopped when he saw Alyssa's face. She'd managed only three eggs and looked close to tears. So David moved behind her and slipped the gold one into her basket. Mother caught his eye over Alyssa's head and winked.

"This is a perfect, perfect day! I love church on Easter! I love everything about it—the new clothes and the butterflies, the white lilies and the lamb cover, the horns, and the singing. And I especially love the eggs. I love being at Your Easter party, God. I had a great time!" David looked up and blew God a kiss.

Look and Listen

The Easter story is recorded near the end of each gospel: Matthew 28:1–15; Mark 16:1–11; Luke 24:1–12; and John 20:1–18. Before you read, tell the children they should listen so they can quiz you when you've finished. Challenge them to ask tough questions.

Jesus should not have died. Romans 6:23 tells us, "For the wages of sin is death, but the gift of God is eternal life in Christ Jesus our Lord." Since Jesus never sinned, He did not get the eternal death penalty. So, before the just law of God, Jesus agreed to take on Himself all the eternal deaths of people who had sinned. On the cross that Good Friday, Jesus took the full punishment of your sin and my sin, every one of the eternal deaths we deserved. He died completely. And when every death was paid, Jesus said, "It is finished."

Jesus didn't have to come back to earth again. But He returned to show us that everything He said was true. He proved that He had conquered sin and death. We can believe the words, "I have been crucified with Christ. ... The life I live in the body, I live by faith in the Son of God, who loved me and gave Himself for me" (Galatians 2:20). Your eternal death is already completed. You now live a *different* life, one that continues in eternal closeness to God and never ends!

Jesus is alive and so are we! You and I will see Jesus just as Mary, Peter, and all the rest did. This is what Christians celebrate every Easter.

God sighting. Easter colors symbolize God's love for us: green—God grows us in His grace; yellow—Jesus is our Sonshine; blue—God gives us heaven; red—Jesus' blood covers our sins; purple—Jesus is the King. Which color's symbol means the most to you today? Ask God to make that color stand out to you this week.

✔ Using crayon, draw white crosses, fish, and butterflies on hard-boiled eggs before dyeing them. Regular food dye dropped in a mixture of half white vinegar and half water makes lovely pastel shades. You can mute your colors by boiling the eggs with onion skins. You can get amazing leaf prints on the eggs if you press small leaves next to the egg and wrap each in fabric before dyeing. The leaf keeps that area white. The same thing happens when you put rubber bands around the eggs before dyeing. You can get rainbow lines by putting lots of rubber bands on and removing several each time you dunk the egg into a lighter dye.

✔ Make an Easter egg centerpiece with empty eggshells. Get seven eggs. Use a pin to prick a hole in each end of each egg. Blow steadily through one hole until the egg is empty. Rinse the fragile shells and let them dry. Glue all the eggs together and print the words "He is not here, He is risen" on the eggs.

✔ Many families serve a pound cake made in the shape of a lamb with the Easter meal. Lamb molds are available from Maid of Scandinavia in Minneapolis. Request their 800 number from information.

✔ Prepare Easter napkins for Easter breakfast by writing "He is risen" on some and "He is risen indeed" on others. Lay out warm outer clothing so you can jump up when the alarm rings the next morning. Sit out on a heavy blanket to watch the sun rise. Then use the napkins as cues for the traditional Easter greeting. Sample hot cross buns and spicy cups of tea to start the day.

✔ My father once showed us a deep red box with a cross-shaped slit in the top. In his hand he had several gray hearts. As he put each heart through the slit, he mentioned a particular bad deed (ones amazingly familiar to us). Then he'd say, "Jesus died to remove this sin from us." When all the hearts were inside, he asked, "What does Jesus do for sinners? Let's look and see." Carefully he lifted off the lid and tilted the bottom of the box. All the hearts were now white! We thought it was magic! When I was older, Dad showed me that there was a small, flat box taped right under the slit. The gray hearts were caught in this box. The white hearts had been there all along. Even now, I remember this symbol of what Jesus did for us.

Go in Peace

Close by singing:

> Jesus Christ is risen today, Alleluia!
> Our triumphant holy day, Alleluia!
> Who did once upon the cross, Alleluia!
> Suffer to redeem our loss. Alleluia!

Lutheran Worship 127

May Day:
God Loves to Surprise Us

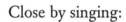

Stop and Think

This is a true story. One evening Pat and I were visiting a family who had agreed to spend time with us to talk about faith in God. Our knock brought the husband, wife, and small daughter to greet us. I was particularly delighted to see the woman's lovely almond eyes and black hair since we'd lived in

Hong Kong many years, and I missed seeing the lovely features of Asian people.

Her name was Ming. She apologized often for her English. I felt a deep bond with her since I'd done my share of apologizing for my Cantonese back in China! Ming had grown up during the Cultural Revolution. She did not practice the worship of the various Chinese gods and ancestor spirits. She grew up with no god at all. She came to America to study at an American university and had met the man who was now her husband. They were both working.

This family had visited our church because Ming felt her daughter needed training in goodness. Like many young families drawn to Christian churches, Ming wanted her daughter surrounded by good examples and kind words. God draws people to Himself in a variety of ways. The surprise is always that when people seek goodness, they can actually find the source of goodness.

At home, as I was praying before I went to bed, Ming's last question stayed with me. She asked, "How can I learn of this Jesus?" Pat had suggested that she get a Bible storybook and read it with her child before bedtime.

So in my prayer I said, "God, if you want me to get Ming a Bible storybook, please get me the money tomorrow in an envelope."

Can you guess what happened the next day? I got $20 in an envelope! I took the money to a Christian bookstore and found two perfect books, a slender one that would help Ming as she began to learn and a nice, fat one that would be helpful in about a year. Together, though, they cost more than the money in the envelope. I thought of putting in some of my own money, but then decided that God had given me just exactly what He wanted me to have for this. So I took only the fat book to the counter. When the clerk rang it up, the register said $10. I showed the clerk the price sticker on the book, but she insisted that the price in the computer was correct.

I said "Just a minute" and grabbed the slender book too.

One more surprise happened. Because it was the week of Chinese New Year, I thought Ming would enjoy a licee packet. In China, people give these small red envelopes as gifts to each other. I pulled out one that I'd saved, and the Chinese character printed there was "double happiness." I think God had been saving that one for a special occasion.

Look and Listen

The May Day tradition of making a flower basket, setting it on someone's porch, and running away is fun to do. May seems to surprise and delight all of us with its scattered colors. Imagine how color would surprise animals who can only see in black and white. Or imagine if we had the visual range of certain animals who see beyond the color spectrum! (Have you ever wondered what kind of sight angels have?) I wonder if we will be surprised by new colors in heaven.

Flowers can surprise us in another way—shape. Just when I think I've seen every possible way God might shape a flower, something totally new comes along. The flat-petaled daisy is completely different from the rose. The rose is completely different from the iris. And who would ever guess that a dandelion would turn into that amazing puff ball!

Even seeds are different. Strawberries have about a hundred on top of the fruit. Pomegranates have about that many inside! A plum only has one, and who'd ever imagine the slippery seed inside the avocado! And who wouldn't be amazed to see what happens to a popcorn seed when it gets hot!

Remember the first time you ever saw a giraffe? Wow! What a surprise! Would you ever have invented the ostrich? Some animals seem to be made to demonstrate God's love of surprises.

Proverbs 8:22–31 tells us that wisdom delights in the surprising marvels of God's creation. Read those verses together.

God sighting. God surprised me with exactly the right amount of money for a double gift. Has God ever surprised you? Ask this question of someone you know. Tell the family what he or she said.

Proceed with Care

- ✔ If you don't have real flowers to pick, tissue flowers are fun and pretty. Peel apart four to six facial tissues into single layers. Lay them carefully on top of one another. Tie the center securely with thread and then gently pull the layers apart to form carnationlike flowers. Set these posies in a homemade basket. An easy basket to make is illustrated here.

- ✔ Figure out ways to surprise each other. Put a note in an odd spot like Dad's wallet or under the windshield wiper of the car. Bring home a surprise gift like a single flower for a child. Surprise someone with a foot rub or by doing his or her chore. Give some unexpected time to one person for an ice-cream cone or a bike ride to a park.

- ✔ Make marshmallow surprises. Cut any sweet dough into triangles. Wrap one triangle around a large marshmallow that you've dipped in melted butter and rolled in cinnamon sugar. Pinch the seams and place each seam-side-down in muffin tins. Let rise about an hour. Bake at 375 degrees for about 10 minutes. Cover with foil the last few minutes so the tops don't get overbrown. Drizzle on icing if you want a really sweet treat!

- ✔ Swap houses with friends for a fancy dining surprise. Set up your own dining table and have supper ready on the stove. Don't tell the children where you're going out to eat. Be sure you've exchanged house keys!

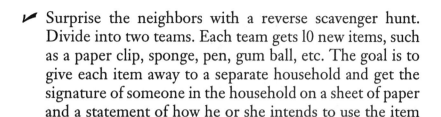

✔ Surprise the neighbors with a reverse scavenger hunt. Divide into two teams. Each team gets 10 new items, such as a paper clip, sponge, pen, gum ball, etc. The goal is to give each item away to a separate household and get the signature of someone in the household on a sheet of paper and a statement of how he or she intends to use the item before going to bed that night!

✔ Cut an apple horizontally to find the surprise hidden inside (a star). Use the apple as a print block by spreading tempera paint on a wet, folded paper towel. Press the apple half onto the paint pad and then onto plain paper. Use the paper as a gift wrap later. Or print the apples in rows across the bottom of some paper place mats your church can use. Be sure to make enough.

Pray this prayer together:

> God makes the clouds rain goodness,
> The deserts bloom and spring,
> The hills leap up in gladness,
> The valleys laugh and sing.
> God fills them with his fullness,
> All things with large increase;
> He crowns the year with blessing,
> With plenty and with peace.

Lutheran Worship 493

Go in Peace

Mother's Day: God Nurtures His Children through Parents and Caregivers

Pastor Glick gathered the children around him on the chancel steps. "Good morning!" he said. "Good to see you here." One little fellow, Nicholas, wriggled in the small slice of space between his brother, Ben, and the pastor.

"I want to talk about birds today," Pastor said. "Have you ever seen baby birds with their mother?"

Nicholas raised his hand. He tilted his face up to Pastor and said, "We had baby birds in our tree last year. They made lots of noise."

"Baby birds make the most noise when the mother comes with food. They open their beaks wide and clamor to eat." Pastor held up a picture of a mother chickadee and her babies. "When the babies are very young, the mother actually eats the food and lets her body turn it into baby food. Then she brings it up to put it in her chicks' bodies."

"Birds make baby food?" Nicholas asked in amazement.

"Yeah, they do. That's the way God makes mother birds. Do you know God makes your parents and those who love you the same way?"

"My mother fed Nicholas baby food once," Ben said. "He liked the bananas but spit out the peas. I remember it."

Before Ben could go on, Pastor steered the conversation back. "Every child up here needs special 'food.' I'm not talking about baby food or vegetables. I'm talking about your spirit's

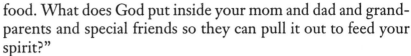

food. What does God put inside your mom and dad and grand-parents and special friends so they can pull it out to feed your spirit?"

The children sat silently. They hadn't thought about food for their spirits before. Pastor Glick pulled a baby food jar from his robe pocket. "What's in here?" he asked. All the children leaned toward the jar.

"Red things," answered Nicholas.

"Candy hearts," answered Ben.

Pastor opened the jar and spilled several cinnamon hearts into his hand. "God put love inside those who care for you so they can pull love out when you need it to feed your spirits. Sometimes your mom will give you a big squeeze and a smoochy kiss. Does she ever do that?"

Nicholas giggled and Ben nodded. He looked into the congregation to see his mother.

"Sometimes your mom will hold you and maybe rock you. Sometimes Dad will carry you up on his shoulders or help you learn to catch a ball. Maybe your special friend who takes care of you after school pours you something to drink and listens while you tell what happened at recess." Several children nodded.

"Now do you think your mom is going to rock you when you're 35 years old or your dad is going to carry you piggyback when you're 40?" Nicholas imagined himself as big as his dad on his dad's shoulders. The image made him giggle even more. "But you know what? God will still be putting love inside your parents and others so they can pull it out and give it to you as food for your spirit. It won't be baby food or children food then. It will be grown-up love. Still, God will make sure that someone gives you His love. That's the way God is. Let's pray."

All the children bowed their heads.

God nurtures us. He invented parenting. God could have designed people like spiders—a whole group of us would hatch together as miniature adults. Or He could have had us be like many plants whose seeds are blown away to grow up far apart.

Instead God wanted us to be loved and thereby learn to love. All love comes from God. The verse "We love because He first loved us" (1 John 4:19) tells us where love comes from. God loves the moms and dads, and then they give love to their children. As children grow, they give love to others too. Timothy's life shows this love. Read about him in 2 Timothy 1:1–7.

Who received God's love from Eunice? Who received love from Lois? Who now also loves Timothy and writes an encouraging letter to him? What three things does Paul say God gives all of us (verse 7)? Timothy was a teenager when he first met Paul. He traveled with Paul on missionary trips. Later Timothy settled down to lead a church in Ephesus. Tradition says Timothy joined Paul in Rome and was even imprisoned but later released. God sent love to Timothy, and from the overflow of love inside Timothy, he was able to love others.

God sighting. Watch for grown-ups and children loving someone this week. Since all love comes from God, then all the loving words and actions you see are also from God. You are witnessing God at work!

Proceed with Care

✔ How well do you know each other? Try out these questions:
1. What really makes your son or daughter angry?
2. Who is Dad or Mom's hero?
3. What color would your child like the bedroom to be?
4. What is Mom's favorite dessert?
5. What is your son's or daughter's biggest fear?

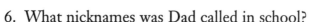

6. What nicknames was Dad called in school?
7. What is each person's favorite Bible verse?
8. What is each person's biggest gripe?
9. What has been the biggest disappointment in your child's life?
10. What gift does your son or daughter most cherish?
11. If each of you had one wish, what would that wish be?
12. What is Dad or Mom's most prized possession?
13. Who outside God and the family loves each of you in very significant ways?
14. What is your child's best memory so far?
15. How many kisses did Mom get so far today?

See how well your family scores by writing answers on paper and comparing them.

✔ Give each child an empty bucket. Dad and Mom get full pitchers of water. Ask the children which words they most like to hear from you. As they say these words, spill some water into the buckets. Then ask what things you do with them that they like the most (back rubs, piggyback rides, etc.). Again, pour water into their buckets as they talk. Continue pouring as they say which presents you've given them and which activities you've done together "feed" them love. Talk about having a full love bucket. Teach them to tell you, "My love bucket is on empty right now," when they need to communicate how they feel. You can say the same on your down days too.

✔ Write "Ten Commandments for a Happy Family." You might include the following: "You shall praise God for giving each family member to the other"; "You shall not lie to one another or speak unkind, untrue criticisms"; or "You shall respect closed doors and request permission to enter a room or use personal belongings."

✔ Make pop-up cards as illustrated. Add an appropriate message from the heart.

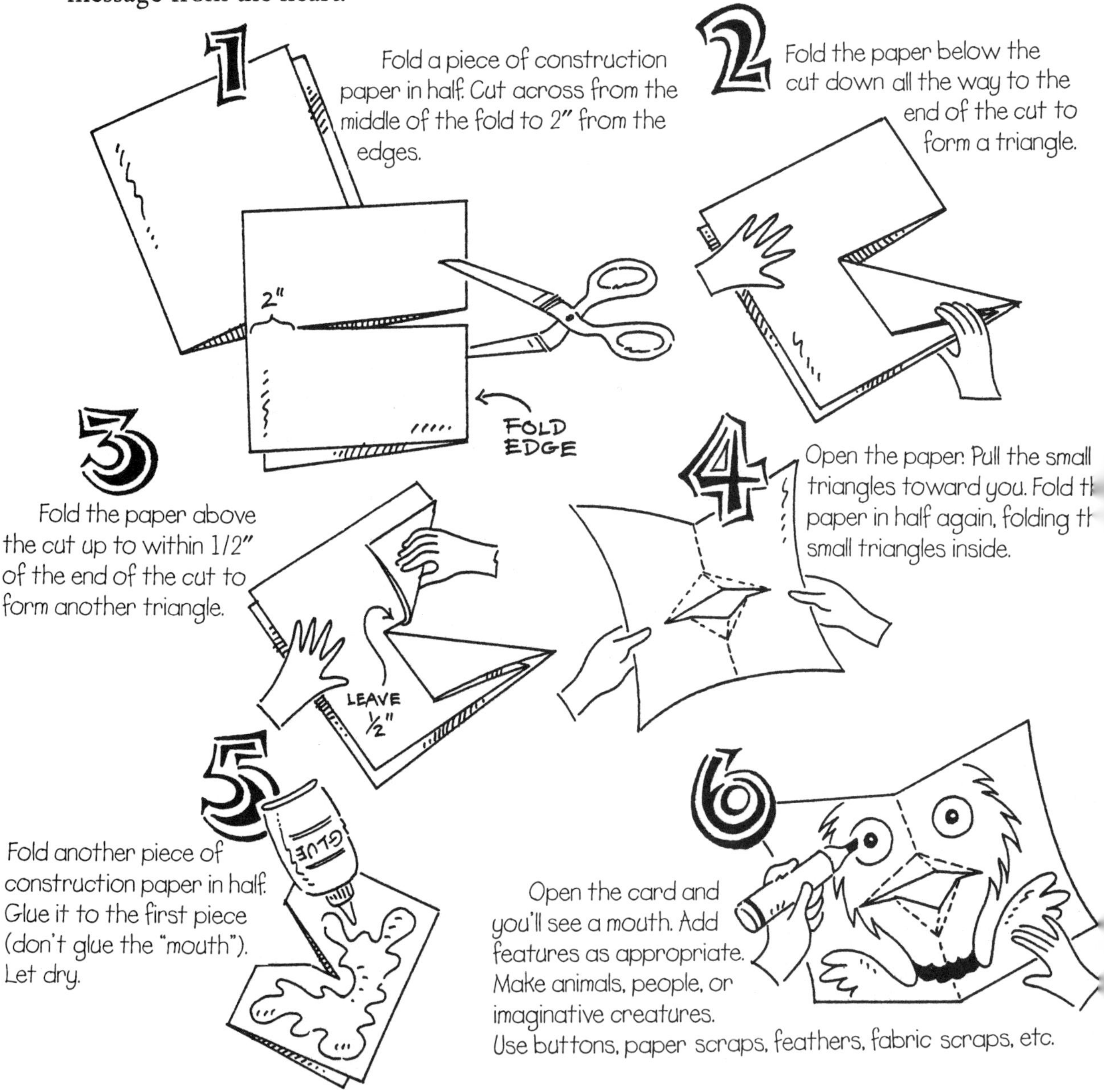

1 Fold a piece of construction paper in half. Cut across from the middle of the fold to 2" from the edges.

2"

FOLD
EDGE

2 Fold the paper below the cut down all the way to the end of the cut to form a triangle.

3 Fold the paper above the cut up to within 1/2" of the end of the cut to form another triangle.

LEAVE
½"

4 Open the paper. Pull the small triangles toward you. Fold the paper in half again, folding the small triangles inside.

5 Fold another piece of construction paper in half. Glue it to the first piece (don't glue the "mouth"). Let dry.

GLUE

6 Open the card and you'll see a mouth. Add features as appropriate. Make animals, people, or imaginative creatures. Use buttons, paper scraps, feathers, fabric scraps, etc.

✔ Since the devotion talked about feeding baby-food love, have a Baby Time. Finger-paint with baby lotion. Taste a jar of baby food. Listen to Mom and Dad croon lullabies, such as "Hush Little Baby" and "Rock-a-bye, Baby." Recite all the nursery rhymes you can remember. Sprinkle baby powder into a box and spell out baby words with your finger. Rub some baby oil on your elbows and knees. Read about Bible babies, such as Moses (Exodus 2:1–10) and John (Luke 1). Get out your baby books and photo albums. Can you see God's love in those times?

Go in Peace

As Mom closes her eyes, let each family member touch her mouth, eyes, ears, hands, arms, knees, or feet as you thank God for what Mom does with that part of her body. (She talks wise words, sees what help you need, listens to your good and bad news, makes things or does things with her hands, gives hugs, prays, or goes to get things for you.)

Pentecost: Jesus Gives Believers the Holy Spirit

Stop and Think

Drew slammed the door and stomped into his room. Soon Mrs. Smith heard banging sounds coming from the room. She knocked on his bedroom door. "Can I come in?"

"Yes," Drew growled. He was rearranging his toy shelf, pushing boxes of Lego blocks and game boxes against the wall.

"Why do I get the feeling you are angry?" asked Mrs. Smith.

"Because I *am* angry," Drew answered hotly. "Do you know what Alex just told me? He said that his friend Joe is his best friend." He shoved another box against the wall.

"Joe? I don't know anyone named Joe."

"That's because there *is* no Joe. Only Alex can see him, he says. How can he be so stupid? He just made Joe up. Mom, it's just so stupid. Nothing is invisible."

"Oh, I wouldn't say that. People aren't invisible, that's true. But there are real invisible things," Mrs. Smith countered.

"Sure, air is invisible. But that's all."

"Well, actually there are lots of invisible things: wind, radio waves, viruses, the colors in a beam of light, oh—and angels."

Drew rolled his eyes. Mrs. Smith put up her hand. "Wait a minute, Drew. This is interesting. Now I know you're upset about Alex making up a friend. Let's leave that a minute and just think about 'invisible' together."

"Okay, it's true what you said about those invisible things you named, except for the viruses. I bet we'll be able to see them some day. But nothing about a person is invisible."

"Not true," answered Mrs. Smith. "Remember the Pentecost story in church? When Peter finished his first sermon, he said that everyone who repented and was baptized in the name of Jesus would receive the gift of the Holy Spirit (Acts 2:38). So inside all those first Christians and inside us today is something invisible—the Holy Spirit."

Drew was intrigued. "What's He doing in there?"

"Actually, the Holy Spirit does quite a few things in you. First of all He brings to your mind what you've learned about God. Sometimes Bible verses that you memorized come into your head, or Christian songs, or Bible stories. The Spirit is always reminding you of the truth. God pours His love into our hearts through the Holy Spirit. Out of this love comes all the fruit the Spirit produces in us, such as joy, peace, patience, kindness … "

"Goodness, faithfulness, gentleness, and self-control," finished Drew. "I know that verse."

"Well, there you go then. The Spirit was working in you just now!" Drew smiled at his mother. "Why do I get the impression you're feeling better now?" she asked.

Drew's eyebrows lifted. "Okay, Mom, we've just talked about some pretty interesting stuff. Still—there's Joe to deal with."

"Remember that I said the Holy Spirit is also called the Spirit of Truth. Maybe you can think about that. The Holy Spirit lives in Alex's heart too."

Look and Listen

The Spirit hovered over the watery chaos before God said, "Let there be light." The Old Testament records many wonderful deeds by people who were filled with the Spirit. But the most amazing things happened when Jesus kept His word and "poured out His Spirit on all people." Only a few select people in the days before Christ received this gift. Starting on Pentecost, the Holy Spirit has been given to every Christian! The fascinating story of this first occurrence is found in Acts 2. (If your children are young, read verses 1–12, 22–24, and 32–41.)

Who was waiting in the house? When the Spirit came into the room, what sound did they hear? What did they see? How did they start talking? To whom was Peter talking? What did he tell these people? How did they respond? What gift did they receive?

If you were there and you heard huge wind sounds but nothing was blowing, and then you saw flames on people's heads around you, how would you feel? When you heard yourself speaking in Chinese or Russian or some other foreign language, what would you think? If you were helping baptize 3,000 people the rest of the day, what would you be thinking before you went to bed?

God sighting. The Holy Spirit works in many ways. During this family time you thought about three ways the Spirit works: recalling God's Word to your mind, speaking the truth to you and others, and demonstrating His presence through signs and wonders. God is always at work. He is working all three of these activities in someone's life right now. Watch this week for those He works in your life.

Proceed with Care

Celebrate Pentecost in the following ways: Draw red flames on your napkins, bake 12 cupcakes with a candle in each to recall the flames of fire on the disciples' heads, serve red food, and display Baptism memorabilia to remind people of the 3,000 new members that started the church.

- Make a dove bowl by shaping clay into a pinch pot. Then flare out various sections to resemble a dove shape. Clay recipe: 1 cup cornstarch, 2 cups baking soda, 1¼ cups water. Cook over medium heat until thickened to dough-like consistency. Cool and knead. Shape.

- Study the work of the Holy Spirit this week. Here are six verses to look at: John 14:16–17; John 16:13–15; Romans 8:26; Matthew 12:28; Ephesians 3:16–19; 1 Thessalonians 1:6.

- Make pinwheels to watch what invisible wind can do. Tie several together as illustrated to make a Pentecost mobile!

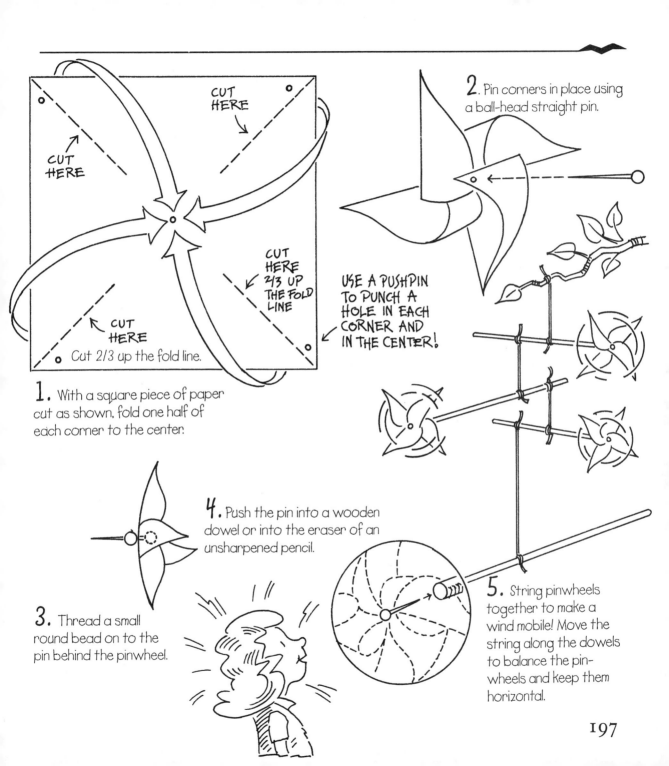

CUT HERE

CUT HERE

CUT HERE

CUT HERE 2/3 UP THE FOLD LINE

CUT HERE

Cut 2/3 up the fold line.

1. With a square piece of paper cut as shown, fold one half of each corner to the center.

2. Pin corners in place using a ball-head straight pin.

USE A PUSHPIN TO PUNCH A HOLE IN EACH CORNER AND IN THE CENTER!

4. Push the pin into a wooden dowel or into the eraser of an unsharpened pencil.

3. Thread a small round bead on to the pin behind the pinwheel.

5. String pinwheels together to make a wind mobile! Move the string along the dowels to balance the pin-wheels and keep them horizontal.

✔ Fool around with some invisible stuff. Fold a sheet of paper into a trough and light a candle. Put ½ cup vinegar into a tall glass. Now add a heaping tablespoon of baking soda to the vinegar. Wait two seconds and then cover the glass with a piece of cardboard. The glass will fill up with carbon dioxide. Carefully tilt the glass and pour the invisible carbon dioxide down the trough onto the lit candle. It will put out the flame. To prove that something other than air was there, relight the candle, and pour an empty glass of air down the trough.

✔ Shatter light into its normally invisible colors by angling a mirror in a bowl of water near a sunny window. This should produce a rainbow on a nearby wall.

Substitute your names into this Bible verse in the appropriate places: "God sent His Son, born of a woman, born under law, to redeem *Drew* ... that *Drew* might receive the full rights of *sons*. Because *Drew* is a *son*, God sent the Spirit of His Son into *Drew's* heart, the Spirit who calls out, *Abba* Father" (Galatians 4:4–6).

Go in Peace

First Day of Summer: God Designed Creation to Praise Him

Matt grabbed his baseball hat and ran past his sister Lara. Lara was dragging a pillow behind her as she read the last page of her book. "Lara, let's go. Stop reading!" called Mom.

Matt was already in the car as Dad strapped down the last of the luggage. Matt stuck his head out the back window and shouted with joy, "School's out! Here we come, Wisconsin!"

Mom locked the front door and clattered down the steps. Soon everyone was buckled in, and they drove off. Every year the Browns rented a cabin on the lake the very first week of summer. Matt and Dad fished, Mom took long nature walks in the woods, and Lara read horse stories. It was blissful!

By late afternoon, the car pulled into the old dirt road that led to the lake. All eyes—even Lara's—feasted on the towering old pines. "There goes a porcupine," pointed Matt.

"Let's see who can spot a deer first," said Mom.

Lara thought about her special secret place, a log in a clearing off to the left of the road. "I wonder if those blue flowers are there this year?" she said.

The car bumped past clumps of Queen Anne's lace and cornflowers. A sparkle from the sun off the lake flashed in less dense areas of the woods. The car rounded a corner and pulled up to an old stone and wood cabin. Matt was on the ground running before the engine switched off.

"Hello cabin! Hello lake! Hello everybody! We're here!" he yelled out to all the inhabitants. His feet clamored up the wooden steps, and he hopped from one foot to the other waiting for Dad to unlock the door.

Dad got out of the car and stretched. He caught Mom's eye and sighed, "I love coming here." They looked at each other with that special loving look, but Matt's insistence broke through.

"Hurry up! Open the door!"

As the parents brought in bedding, groceries, and supplies, Matt and Lara raced around. Finally Mom laughed and said, "Off with you then." Both dashed outside—Matt to the lake to see if he could skip rocks better this year since he'd grown and Lara to check if her secret spot was still there.

After things were in place, Mr. and Mrs. Brown started on a stroll along one of the back trails. They walked arm in arm. "I love the smells out here. The sky seems cleaner and the earth smells fresher," Dad said.

"You know what I think it is," Mom said, "I think at home, everything is in straight lines. I mean, think about it. Houses are straight lines. Sidewalks are straight lines. Even roads are mostly straight lines! But look here. Those trees are tall but not exactly straight lines. This path is anything but straight. I don't think God was into straight lines when He created the earth."

Mr. Brown, a science teacher, answered, "I don't know. Light travels in a straight line. And crystals are all straight from snow crystals to diamonds."

"Yes, but I can name hundreds of animals and trees that you couldn't say are straight," debated Mrs. Brown.

They heard a crashing in the underbrush on their left.

Matt charged them! "Mom, Dad, I saw the first deer. It was awesome!" As soon as he said this, he whirled around and raced back.

"Well, that child sure travels in straight lines," chuckled Dad. "Beelines."

Look and Listen

Everything in our universe is incredible—from the tiny flowers that bloom in summer to the billowing clouds resting in the blue expanse of an Oklahoma sky. What do you love in nature that is straight? not straight? yellow? red? smooth? bumpy? invisible? musical? What smell delights you? What tastes?

Everything on earth is designed to praise the Creator. Look at Psalm 148 together.

Name some of God's creations that the psalmist was exhorting to praise God. Did you see grandfathers in verse 12? Did you notice kids are mentioned (verse 12)?

You know, God could have made only plants. There are so many of them; surely He gets lots of praise from them. Why did He add animals to His creation? What unique praises do they add?

With all the joyful noise of animals, why would God add humans to His creation? What unique praises do we add?

God sighting. Ask God to show you something beautiful that He created to praise Him. Then watch to see what this treasure is. When you find it, tag it "Made by God."

Proceed with Care

✔ In one of the books in the Chronicles of Narnia series by C. S. Lewis there's an account of creation that is delightful. Begin the first book of the series, *The Lion, the Witch, and the Wardrobe*, during this family time.

- Build a birdhouse together for wrens or other creatures of God that you'd like to observe.

- Make leaf boats by curling up the edges of large leaves. Float them in nearby water or puddles that have been created by the rain that praises God.

- Take an ABC hike. Give each person a piece of paper marked with the letters A through Z. Challenge the family to spot one nature item per letter as you walk in the park or woods.

- God separated the water and the land. Lay a yardstick or string on the floor. Call one side "the bank" and the other side "the water." Start with everyone on the bank. Then call "in the water." Everyone should jump to the other side. Randomly call out one of the phrases and see who can keep track correctly of where to jump—straight up or over the line. (Call directions quickly for older children.)

- Play Animal, Vegetable, Mineral. The first player writes the name of something on a piece of paper. The rest of the family can ask 20 questions in order to guess the word. All questions may only be answered with "yes" or "no" by the player. The first question is often something like, "Is it an animal?"

As one person rereads Psalm 148, the rest can pantomime it as a motion prayer. Try it as a round-robin, a whole group effort, or a combination of the two.

Go in Peace

Father's Day:
God Provides and Protects
His Children through Parents

Stop and Think

Mr. Behning rubbed the back of his neck. Then he swallowed some more coffee. "This isn't what they hired me to do. I'd never have taken a job like this. I don't like traveling. I don't like sales. But you can bet if I don't take this, the next time layoffs roll around, my name will be on the list."

Mrs. Behning put her hand over her husband's hand. "You're seeing a pretty gloomy picture up ahead."

Mr. Behning nodded. "I feel so trapped."

They both heard the bus pull up to the corner house. In less than a minute their three kids brought lively noise through the front door. The two oldest continued bantering about yesterday's skating practice. The youngest dragged a book bag toward her room. "Ann, how was your day?" asked her mother.

Ann let the bag drop and looked solemnly at her mother's face. Then she noticed her daddy was home. He held out his arms, sensing some kind of second-grade troubles. Ann moved into his arms and was soon on his lap. She didn't seem surprised to see her dad home early.

"What's going on with my favorite second-grader?" he asked.

"Gayla Hardy is moving."

Mr. and Mrs. Behning eyed each other over Ann's head. Gayla's father was laid off his job six months ago. He hadn't been able to find work. His wife took a clerking job at the drugstore, but the Behnings knew the family couldn't keep up the mortgage without Mr. Hardy's salary.

"Daddy, every time I have a friend, she moves away. Without Gayla, there won't be anything to do at recess."

Mr. Behning hugged his little daughter and then said, "I'll pray about all this in my prayers tonight. Then we'll talk some more. I know God loves us, Ann. He loves Gayla too. He'll work out something." He paused. "Do you want a piece of my doughnut to sweeten the day?"

Ann took a bite, then another. "Leave some for me, you silly Willy!" said Daddy. Ann gave her dad a sugary kiss on the cheek and jumped down. As she headed for the kitchen, she called back, "Love you, Daddy."

Mrs. Behning smiled at her husband. "You do such a good job as a dad. The kids really know you love them. Someday they'll realize all that you sacrifice for them to provide their home." She got up to clear away the coffee cups and doughnut crumbs. But when she moved to Mr. Behning's side of the table, he grabbed her around the waist.

"Hey," she laughed. "I'm going to drop this."

"Set it down a minute."

"What are you up to?" asked Mrs. Behning as she put the cups back on the table. Mr. Behning pulled her onto his lap. "You make me feel young again," said Mrs. Behning smiling.

"You know something, Beth. It helps to know that, even though the kids may not see all that I do to provide for them and protect them, you see it."

"Well, of course, I see it! You're a good man, Fred. You're a godly man. And I'll tell you what—I'll pray about the department switch for you in my prayers tonight. Then we'll talk some more. I know God loves us. He can manage this."

Mr. Behning gave his wife a kiss before she got up to clean the coffee cups.

Look and Listen

St. Paul never had children, but he did have younger people he called sons because they'd become dear to him. He'd taken over the position of providing for and protecting them. One of these young people, Onesimus, had run away from his owner. In those days, if a runaway slave was caught, he was usually killed. God brought this young person to Paul, who at that time was in a Roman jail. Paul became like a father to Onesimus and helped him understand that he could not run all his life. Paul wrote a letter to Onesimus' owner, Philemon. He crafted his letter so carefully that Philemon could hardly refuse Paul's request. Read the letter in the New Testament book, Philemon.

What did Paul immediately remind Philemon of in verse 1? What did he call Philemon in that verse? What compliments did Paul make of Philemon in verses 5 and 7? What does Paul call Onesimus in verses 10 and 12? Notice his persuasion in verses 13 and 14. What does he want Philemon to do for Onesimus in verse 16? Onesimus probably stole from Philemon. How does Paul provide for this in verse 19? Finally, to be sure all went well for Onesimus, what does Paul suggest in verse 22? (Think of Jesus saying verses 10–18 to God the Father on Judgment Day with you standing at His side. Wow!)

God designed families. He placed parents, particularly fathers, in the role of provider and protector. Dads model what God the Father does for us, His children. We honor fathers and the sacrifices they make out of love on this special day of the year.

God sighting. Use the phrase this week, "I'll pray about this in my prayers tonight." Try to make this a commonly heard phrase in your home.

✔ Plan to shine all Dad's shoes during family time or wash his car inside and out.

✔ Make Dad a briefcase card like the one illustrated:

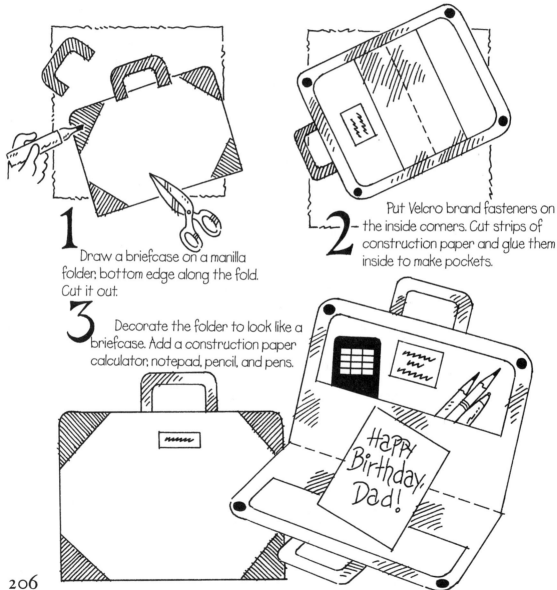

1 Draw a briefcase on a manilla folder, bottom edge along the fold. Cut it out.

2 Put Velcro brand fasteners on the inside corners. Cut strips of construction paper and glue them inside to make pockets.

3 Decorate the folder to look like a briefcase. Add a construction paper calculator, notepad, pencil, and pens.

Happy Birthday, Dad!

✓ Have each child pick a place to hide. Then make up clues to give to Dad. The first clue leads to the youngest child who holds the next clue.

✓ Stage a show for Dad on his special day. Have each person carry some item of Dad's like a baseball glove, sock, or a garden tool and sing a song about it. Use the tune for "Happy Birthday to You" or "For He's a Jolly Good Fellow." Finish with a spirited, "Yea, Dad" cheer!

✓ Let each person tell the funniest thing he or she has ever seen Dad do.

✓ Quiz Dad with these questions:
1. Where were you when I was born?
2. Have you ever grown a beard or mustache?
3. Which piece of clothing do you dislike?
4. What was your favorite book in grade school?
5. Did you ever get in trouble with your dad?
6. If you had lots of time and money, what would we do on vacation?

✓ Outline Dad's hands on a large piece of paper. Write or draw pictures of all the things Dad does for the family with his hands.

✓ Have a "Let's Dress up Dad" time. Limit materials to fabric pieces, sheets, and towels for one ensemble. Then try another with aluminum foil and paper grocery bags. Make the final one with just toilet paper.

✓ Decorate a Daddy Date Book with photos of each of the children. This is the place to keep souvenirs from each place where Dad takes a child on a date. This can be the wrapper from a straw at the ice-cream shop or the zoo entrance stub. If you encourage each child to write a comment beside the souvenir, you'll have a keepsake.

Surround Dad, hold hands, and pray:

> Our Father, by whose name
> All fatherhood is known,
> Who dost in love proclaim
> Each family thine own,
> Bless thou all parents, guarding well,
> With constant love as sentinel,
> The homes in which thy people dwell.

Lutheran Worship 465

Go in Peace

Independence Day: God Gives Us Government & Authority

Once upon a time the new king of Pridania said, "Good citizens, on the death of my father, I have taken the oath as king to lead you to new triumphs. I have decided many of the former policies were overly harsh and must be changed!" The crowd below his balcony cheered.

"I have decided, with the counsel of my new advisors, that from henceforth, all laws are abolished." More cheers. "All prisoners will be set free, and no one will ever have to fear again!" The crowd went wild.

"Do what you know in your hearts is good. Do what is right in your own eyes. Go now in peace!"

The crowd cheered uproariously—and then broke into the old king's wine cellar.

Stop and Think

The young king's burly guards prevented the mob from stealing most of the palace furniture by well-placed thumps and whacks.

Dismayed, the new king nervously muttered, "They're just so happy that they aren't thinking clearly. Tomorrow will be better."

The next day things were more normal except for the 1,000 police officers without jobs. Without laws there was nothing to enforce. The judges in the kingdom also set their robes aside and considered other government functions until they realized, along with the firefighters, that without laws, no one would have to pay taxes.

The following day post offices all over the kingdom shut down and the public school teachers began to gather in the hallways after school.

Newspapers ran stories about recently released, long-time thieves pulling a string of robberies in one area. A fire in another area had ignited a whole subdivision before rain put out the blaze. Store lootings filled an entire page. The most ominous news came on the editorial page. The former ambassador to the neighboring kingdom, Ravenswood, predicted war.

Gun store sales soared, and grocery stores couldn't keep food stocked because citizens began hoarding for fear of escalating prices. Groups began meeting at night. Some met with concerns to improve the situation with voluntary cooperation lists. Other, less civic-minded, people met to plot their raids on the helpless.

Things went from bad to worse in Pridania. Several times the new king narrowly missed an arrow or a sword as rebels attempted to take his place. Good people banded together and barricaded their homes.

Finally, the new king secretly brought the old king's chief advisor to the palace. He arrived late at night and was delivered promptly to the Council Chamber. The young king sat at the long table chewing his nails. He jumped up eagerly when the older man arrived. Remembering his position, the king sat back down with exaggerated dignity and motioned the older man to a chair. The old man sat down heavily and said nothing.

"Heh, well, hmm," began the young king. "I find myself in need of some advice."

On July 4 we remember that our country declared its independence from England. There were still to be many more meetings by these leaders to establish a new confederation. It didn't take long for the leaders to realize that the United States of America would never survive without a strong common law. In 1787 our Constitution was complete. Since that time, all laws in this country must conform to that document. A democracy is not a government without laws. We have seen many newspaper accounts of what happens to countries when the laws are ignored and people do what is right in their own eyes.

Are all laws good then? The answer isn't a simple yes or no. The apostle Paul wrote to the Christians at the center of the Roman government—the same government whose soldiers beat Jesus and pounded the nails into His hands and feet. The Roman government taxed its people cruelly and spent the money on themselves. Yet look at Paul's words in Romans 13:1–7.

Notice that Paul says Christians are to submit to the government in verse 5. Why? What does he mean when he says "because of conscience"? If the government is corrupt like the Roman government was, did Paul say we could stop paying (verses 6–7)?

God allows various governments to exist, even ones that do not treat people justly. People can work to change the laws, but we are still commanded to submit. We discuss and disagree about exactly when to refuse a government order, but we all understand that we need laws to curb people from temptation and evil.

On July 4 we thank God for the courage of our early founders who gave their time, talents, fortunes, and even their lives to provide a strong country with just laws. On this day we also pray for those involved in our government.

God sighting. Recite this familiar section of the Declaration of Independence, "We hold these truths to be self-evident: that all men are *created* equal; that they are *endowed by their Creator* with certain unalienable rights; that among these are life, liberty, and the pursuit of happiness."

What did these founders believe about God? Our early leaders were God-fearing people, and our laws reflect their beliefs.

Proceed with Care

✔ Sing historic songs, such as our national anthem, "God Bless America," and "My Country 'tis of Thee." If you don't have a local parade, invite the neighbors to have a neighborhood parade complete with decorated bikes, doll buggies, and dressed-up pets.

✔ Be sure to wear red, white, and blue all day. See who can draw the flag from memory. (How many stripes? Which color starts the stripes on top?) Challenge each family member to come up with a different fact about the Revolutionary period.

✔ One of the great blessings we've been given in this country is the Bill of Rights. Name some of our rights. (We have the right to gather in a church, to say what we believe, to choose our own professions, to travel in and out of the country.) If you have a history book, look in the back for the Constitution. It ends with the Bill of Rights.

✔ Make a whizz popper as illustrated for a surprisingly loud pop!

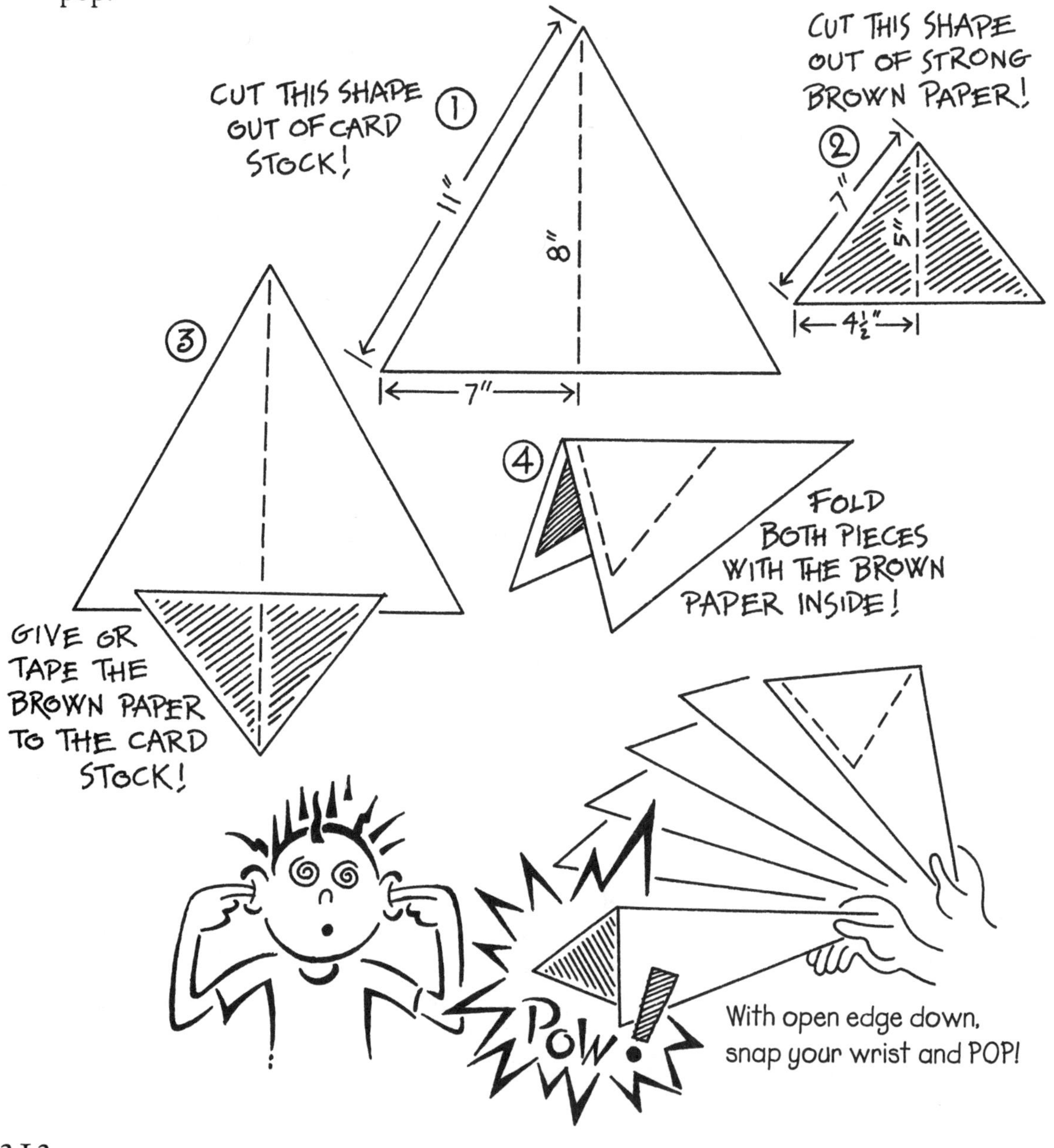

CUT THIS SHAPE OUT OF CARD STOCK!

① 1" 8" 7"

CUT THIS SHAPE OUT OF STRONG BROWN PAPER!

② 7" 5" |← 4½" →|

③

GIVE OR TAPE THE BROWN PAPER TO THE CARD STOCK!

④ FOLD BOTH PIECES WITH THE BROWN PAPER INSIDE!

POW!

With open edge down, snap your wrist and POP!

- Pretend you have been captured by aliens. They can decode your language and seem unlikely to harm you. Yet you realize they want to take you back to their world. Convince them you want to stay on earth—and specifically in America.
- Teach your children to braid using red, white, and blue rug yarn.
- Give each child a detergent bottle filled with red, blue, or clear water. Stand them behind a line that is about three feet away from a set of tin cans. Have each child try to squirt the water into one of the cans. The person with the most water in his or her can wins.
- Play Capture the Flag. Divide the yard into two areas by laying down a rope or spilling a line of white baby powder on the grass. Plant one flag at the back line of each area. The object of the game is to capture the opponent's flag. Players on enemy territory may be tagged. They are then considered captured and must stay in an area you designate as "jail" until they can be tagged by one of their teammates.
- Weave place mats using red and white strips through blue paper that you've slit almost to the edge on each side.

Go in Peace

Drive to your local courthouse, police station, post office, fire station, or other government building. Ask God to give strength, courage, and wisdom to the people who work in that building. Also ask God to help the Christian workers be successful in their witness about our Lord, Jesus Christ.

First Day of School:
Jesus Grew in Knowledge, Stature, and Favor with God and Man

Stop and Think

Tanya zipped her new book bag shut. Looking around her brother, Alec, she pleaded, "Mom, hurry!"

Mrs. Owens grabbed her purse and bustled the two kids out the door into the car. Both poked at each other and talked louder than usual. Mrs. Owens put a Bible story audiocassette in the tape player. Someone had suggested this as a calming way to start the day. It worked too—soon everyone in the car, even Mrs. Owens was absorbed. The storyteller had a pleasant voice.

"Jesus went to year-round school, and He had the same teacher all the time. Of course, school stopped at 10:00, and He had a five-hour lunch."

"Five-hour lunch!" mouthed Alec to Tanya.

"Jesus didn't take a notebook and pencils to school. As a young boy He wrote with a short pointed stick in the sand. As he grew older, He wrote on a wax- or clay-covered slate. He learned to read from scrolls and usually started with Leviticus 1–8. You can see what those chapters are about in your Bibles at home. Jesus probably memorized these verses along with others and had to stand to recite them aloud. Then He sat back down on the floor with the other boys. Notice I didn't say 'boys and girls.' Girls usually didn't go to school."

Alec gave Tanya a smug look.

"At about ten o'clock in the warmer months Jesus would go home. His mother probably already had the barley bread rising, and Jesus may have been sent to gather fuel for the small stone

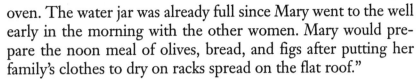

oven. The water jar was already full since Mary went to the well early in the morning with the other women. Mary would prepare the noon meal of olives, bread, and figs after putting her family's clothes to dry on racks spread on the flat roof."

"No drier, Mom," said Tanya.

"Jesus may have waved to His mom and helped her climb down the outside ladder of their house. As He passed through the doorway, Jesus touched the mezuzah and said the special prayer hidden inside. Then He probably grabbed a cloth to help Joseph as he smoothed the wood of a plow handle or brace. After lunch Jesus had some time to play. Ring toss and pitch-the-stone were games of skill. Jesus didn't score in soccer or basketball, but He may have been pretty good with a slingshot."

"No soccer!" thought Alec. "How can you have fun without soccer? Wow—no video games either." Alec was lost in thought for a minute.

"Jesus went back to school at 3:00 and worked on math and history. He also sang in the choir—a boys choir, of course. They sang from the hymnbook of those days, the psalms. I wonder if Jesus had a good voice."

"Mom, can I join choir?" Tanya suddenly asked. "I forgot about it. Ashley and I decided to try out this year. Is that okay?"

"Okay by me if we can figure out a ride home."

The tape continued. "Jesus went home for supper, which was the big meal then. He probably had memory work, and I imagine Jesus studied for tests just like you do."

"Don't mention tests," muttered Alec. Then he caught sight of the school building. His buddy, Adam, was already waving. Both kids snapped open their doors and were gone with a quick kiss.

Mrs. Owens turned off the tape, thinking, I wonder if Jesus' mother felt as proud as I do to have the kids growing up and doing well in school?

Most of Jesus' life in His elementary school years is condensed into two verses: Luke 2:40 and 52. Read them.

Are you growing in stature and strength? How do you think Jesus accomplished that? Be sure to see the last part of verse 40 for the major reason you grow so well.

Are you growing in wisdom? How do you think Jesus accomplished that? (He listened to His teacher and worked very hard; He learned from His parents; He watched other kids play and noticed what helped and what didn't; He studied passages like Proverbs 1:7.)

Are you growing in "favor with man"? Jesus accomplished that the same way kids do today. He took turns. He let others be first sometimes. He helped when someone needed a suggestion or another player on the team. He studied but didn't boast. He laughed when everyone thought something was funny. He didn't put others down. He gave a compliment when a person really did well. You could depend on Him because He kept His word.

Are you growing in favor with God? What would Jesus do to please His Father? (He talked to God in prayer, studied God's Word, did what God told Him to do, thought of others as more important than Himself and served them, cared about anyone and everyone.) A good question to ask yourself whenever you wonder what to do is: What would Jesus do?

God sighting. The next time a situation comes up where your sister has irritated you, someone cut you off in traffic, or someone has just hinted at juicy gossip, ask yourself, What would Jesus do? See if asking God to help you answer that question makes a difference. Do you think it will?

216

TRY WRITING YOUR NAME FROM RIGHT TO LEFT~ LIKE I DID!

Whittle a stick to a point. Roll out play dough or clay on a flat surface like a cake pan or counter top. Then write Jesus' name the way He wrote it. (See illustration.) Try it again by rubbing any dark-colored crayon on paper. Press hard. Then write Jesus' name with a nail. The nail reminds us that Jesus came to earth to die for our salvation.

Jesus often helped His earthly father, Joseph, and His mother, Mary. He also helped neighbors and friends. Trace your hand on a paper plate and cut out the outline. Use a crayon to write your name on one side and "I'll lend you a hand" on the other. Glue the hand to a straw. Make several more and put them into a flowerpot of sand or a tissue box. The type of help you are offering dictates what kind of container you will use.

As a child, Jesus probably played with a toy called a dreidel. Make a spinner out of 4″ × 4″ tagboard. Draw two diagonal lines crisscrossing the square. Print N, G, H, and S in the triangles formed by the lines. Stick a sharp stick through the center. The N stands for "nun" and means you win everything in the center. G means "gimel," and you get half the counters in the center. H is "heh" and means you pass. S is "shin." If you spin and land on S, you must put a counter into the center. Everyone starts with 15 counters. (Use pinto beans or peanuts.) Take turns until someone is out of counters. At that point you can call the one who has the most counters the winner.

✔ Jesus memorized many Bible verses in school. Put the words of these verses on cards. Then make a chart and keep track of which ones each person in your family can say to each other: Psalm 86:5; Psalm 145:18; Leviticus 19:18; Isaiah 56:7; Psalm 107:1; Psalm 92:1; and Psalm 122:1.

✔ Find Nazareth on a Bible map. Sketch a larger map of Israel and mark Nazareth (where Jesus grew up), Bethlehem (Jesus' birthplace), and Jerusalem (where He died). Add the Jordan River (where Jesus was baptized). You can make this a relief map if you put your paper on a board and use clay to add the mountain and valley areas. Jerusalem and Nazareth were both on hills.

✔ Roleplay various familiar situations you've found your-selves in this summer. Then replay the scene. Have some-one call out: What would Jesus do? All of us need to prac-tice being loving, kind, and grace-full so that those responses come easily for us.

Make a scroll. (Roll up a piece of paper and attach a stick to each end.) Let each person in your family write two areas he or she hopes God will grant His grace for improvement this year. Maybe you'd like to be more consistent with homework, with math facts, with good manners, or with kindness. Roll up the scroll and seal it. Have everyone put one hand on the scroll as you ask God, together, to help you grow this year in these ways. Hang it up in a noticeable place like a bathroom or by a back door as a reminder.

Go in Peace

Labor Day:
God Has a Plan for Us

Stop and Think

A. J. rested his cheek on his hand, his head turned sideways towards his father. Dad was grilling bratwurst and corn on the cob. A. J.'s normal enthusiasm for food of any kind was noticeably absent.

"You don't seem too chipper, Buddy," said Dad. "The day is perfect, I'm off work, and you're off school. There's a fresh apple pie waiting in the house, and the Voights will be here later for a friendly game of baseball. How about that!"

A. J. pulled his arm closer in and put his cheek on his knuckles. He slumped deeper into the lawn chair.

"Must be pretty serious if the sizzle of these sausages and the thought of playing ball with Ken doesn't grab you."

"Nothing will help tomorrow, Dad. I'll just have to go back to old Mrs. Hubbel's class and be all by myself."

Dad was quiet a minute and then said, "So you aren't happy to be in that class."

A. J. put both arms on the chair's metal armrests. "How could anybody be happy there? Ken got Mr. O'Connell. They do all the fun stuff. Everybody knows they'll talk all about sports and play math relays and toss a ball around for spelling. What do we do in my class—nothing! All Mrs. Hubbel ever does is make you write, write, write. I'm no good at writing. I hate it."

"Sounds like things are pretty dismal—missing out on Mr. O'Connell and having to do writing. I suppose you feel left out," Dad said.

"I am!" A. J. answered.

"Actually, I don't think so. I can see that you're very disappointed, but for some reason, God wants you in Mrs. Hubbel's class."

A. J. looked puzzled. "What does God have to do with it?"

Dad moved the brats around and turned the corn cobs over. Dad always arranged things carefully so their dinner would be perfectly cooked.

"A. J., God has everything to do with your life. He has plans for you. Look back a bit. Last year you really took off in reading because Mrs. Blomgren got you going on that horse series. You met Ken in that class, remember? You two played this whole summer. If you'd been in someone else's class, that probably wouldn't have happened."

A. J. remembered Mrs. Blomgren. She was wonderful. She told stories with puppets, and they even had a puppet show with puppets they'd made from paper bags. Then he thought of frowning Mrs. Hubbel in her long print dresses and thick brown shoes. He couldn't imagine anything nice from her.

Dad continued, "Remember when we moved here and you were sure nothing good would ever come again? I can still see you pulling your tricycle out of the garage and telling me you were headed back to Oklahoma." Dad chuckled. "But this place has turned out all right, after all."

"Yeah, until now," A. J. groaned.

"I think you need to remember that God has plans for your whole life, A. J. He has 'plans for your good' like the Bible says. Maybe there's some writing talent in you that God wants to bring out." A. J. looked skeptical.

Dad continued, "Well, whatever it is, I know that God put you just where you need to be. I'm going to ask you at the end of this year if you have figured out why God put you in Mrs. Hubbel's class. I bet you that some surprises will happen. Now, go get me a plate for all this food, and let's eat!"

Look and Listen

Read Jeremiah 29:11 and Psalm 139:16. The Bible mentions three effects of God's plans in the first passage. What will His plans give us? (Prosperity, hope, and a future.) What might "prosper you"? (Learning to be disciplined with time, compassionate with others, patient, and hard-working.) What might "give you hope and a future"? (Knowing God came through in my past experiences and will again, being confident that Jesus has given me salvation and heaven.) From the Psalm passage, when did God make His plans for each of us?

Many stories in the Bible illustrate how God's plans work out for good. Read about a man in John 9. You might think God messed up on this man. After all, he was blind at a time when people believed this meant either he or his parents had been punished by God (verse 34). Still, God made sure this man was born a Jew and regularly attended the synagogue. When Jesus came to this man's town, not only did this man begin to see like you and I do, but he also met Jesus in person!

Then the Pharisees bullied the formerly blind man and even told him he couldn't worship in the synagogue anymore! But Jesus came back to find him. Look what happened in verse 38! God gave this man prosperity, hope, and a future.

God sighting. Reflect on the last year or two of your lives. Can you see God's plan unfolding? Be specific. Has He developed some aspect of your character or skills? Has He given you good things or experiences? Do you have hope that He will continue to keep His hand in your life? Does your future seem pleasing to you?

✔ Make paper-bag puppets for the John 9 story. Fill lunch-size bags with shredded newspaper. Insert a dowel or stick in the opening of the bags and tightly tie a string around each bag to form a neck. Make sure the stick extends out enough for your child to grip. Add facial features with construction paper, buttons, yarn, etc., as illustrated.

✔ Make some special foods today. An apple pie is a tradition with many families. Let the kids slice the apples and measure out a ½ cup each of flour, sugar, and butter for the crumb topping.

✔ If you have company over, play Steal the Bacon. Divide the group into two teams. Line up about 10 to 20 yards apart facing a chair placed between the two teams. Put a handkerchief on the chair. Then starting from the end nearest the caller, give each member of Team A a number, beginning with the number 1. Starting from the end farthest from the caller, give each member of Team B a number, also beginning with the number 1. When the caller yells, "Three," the number 3 player from Team A and the number 3 player from Team B run out and try to grab the handkerchief. A point is scored if the person can get back to the team's boundary line without getting tagged by the other called player.

- ✔ Bring items home from work or school to show your family. How are these items used? Who helped us develop the skill to use them? Pantomime various jobs for family members to guess. Along with the familiar firefighter, police officer, doctor, astronaut, and teacher, also add homemaker, landscaper, park ranger, grocery checker, pastor, and others your family would recognize.

- ✔ TV viewing time can be earned by trading it equally with time spent working: chores, practicing piano, or homework. Set up a chart to record the minutes each child has accumulated and keep track of how much time he or she actually spends in front of the TV. Start a new chart every week.

Go in Peace

Tie a long string between two chairs. On the left half of the string, clip index cards describing the order of events in your lives so far. Leave the right half empty to represent your future. We don't know our whole time line but God does. Repeat Jeremiah 29:11. Then praise God for making plans for your family for the rest of your lives!

First Day of Fall: God Makes Aging Beautiful

Stop and Think

Leaning back on the porch rail, I studied my grandmother's profile. She was perched on an old wooden rocker, holding her Bible three inches from her eyes. Her head trembled slightly as she read. It always did. Everything about her seemed soft—from the peach fuzz covering her face to her plump ankles. She wore sturdy black granny shoes, but they weren't shiny. Nothing was shiny, just soft and quiet.

I must have made a noise because she looked up and then around. She squinted and then saw me. I knew the moment she recognized me because all her wrinkles exploded into that beaming smile I love so much.

"Child," she chirped. "How delightful that you're here." She laid her tatted lace bookmark slowly in place and closed the Bible. As she reached for her cane, I was by her arm.

"Don't get up, Grandma. It's just me." I spoke loudly and slowly because that's the way Mama showed me.

Grandma let her hands relax on the rocker and her weight fall back. She had brown spots on her arms, and her skin seemed thin and delicate. I could see blue veins.

She reached out her hand and stroked my cheek. "Carolyn, you sweet child. Did you come to keep me company? Shall we play something?"

"Let's play hide-and-seek. I'll hide first." I loved this game but had to think quickly. The last time we played, she found me every time. I'd be trickier this time! "Okay, ready!"

Grandma called, "Are you in the kitchen?"

I giggled. "No."

"Are you in the bedroom upstairs?"

"Nope!"

"Hmm. You are tricky. Are you in the laundry room?"

Close, I thought. "Yes, but you have to guess where," I answered.

"Laundry room, laundry room," she mumbled. Then her face lit up. "You're in the hamper!"

"You found me," I cried. "Here's your kiss." I kissed her soft cheek and then rubbed my own against it. Just then, Kristen from next door came running across the yard, pigtails flying.

"Carolyn! Can you play?" she hollered from down on the lawn. We usually played whenever we visited Grandma. "Hello Mrs. Murray," she called up.

My grandmother smiled at both of us. "I'm so glad you can be friends to each other." She patted my hand and said, "Off with you then."

"Let's rake up the leaves and jump in them!" Kristen whooped. I began dashing right after her but just before going around the corner, I looked back. Grandma was reaching for her Bible. The light slanted across her old porch and just caught the side of her face. I think my grandmother is the most beautiful person I know. She is full of gentle light. She is full of love.

Look and Listen

What did Solomon, the wisest man on earth, say in Ecclesiastes 3:1? God is changing His creation all the time! As His handiwork ages, much of it becomes more and more beautiful. A street arched with old elms or oaks in summer is lovely and cool, but the same street in autumn is an artist's pallet! Pick up a single leaf and count the shades of color you find there!

Animals age too, moving from their cute early days to mature, full-coated majesty. Think of the early fawn that becomes a stately buck moving through the woods.

How does God age humans into more and greater beauty? If we define beauty the way advertising does, your grandma wouldn't win against Miss America, would she? Grandpa probably doesn't have the biceps of Mr. Atlas or the hair of your favorite singer either. But which of these would you rather sit near on a crisp fall evening by a flickering fire, roasting marshmallows? Whose face is more dear to you?

Not every person ages well. There's a saying: People either mature into fine wine or sour into vinegar. C. S. Lewis once described an older woman as a "Grumble." She'd complained so much during her life that, finally, the only thing left was her grumpy, gravelly grumble. Whether we age into fine-wine people or into vinegar people is pretty much up to how we let Jesus fill the places in our hearts. The more Jesus can act as that marvelous spring of life welling up in our hearts, the more sparkling and beautiful we become to those around us.

God sighting. Your skin isn't like a baby's skin anymore, is it? Which skin would you prefer on the playground or while you wash dishes? Your hair isn't like baby hair. Which would you prefer on a brisk evening walk home? God is growing your "outside," but how is He growing your inside, your spirit?

 **Proceed with Care**

- Collect leaves and small flowers. Press them between pages of a catalog or newspaper with books stacked for weight. Arrange them on waxed paper and then place another piece over the top. Iron the two together and hang this ornament in a sunny window. You can also make bookmarks by sealing small leaves, ferns, and flowers in clear vinyl adhesive paper. Punch a hole in the top and loop ribbon for a tassel. Use any leftovers for potpourri in the bathroom this week.

- Wash red apples and cut each vertically into $\frac{1}{8}$" circles. Let the circles dry or dehydrate them. Hot-glue the most uniform ones to a 9" wire circle or ring of cardboard. Thread bright berries around the apples and tie with a red or brown ribbon for a fall wreath!

- How many words can you rhyme with fall? After you've created a good list, make up a four-line poem. Tack it on the tree nearest the kitchen window.

- Gather up snapshots of relatives and friends. Turn them upside down in the center of the table. Take the top picture and see if other family members can guess your person within five questions. You might also use these pictures for prayer blessings.

- Make the first day of fall a tradition! Stuff an old pair of your dad's trousers and a shirt full of leaves. Add a paper-bag face, yarn beard, and hat. Let your leaf man sit on a porch chair for the annual fall family photo. If your town allows leaf burning, add some to a few logs in a bare spot in the backyard. (Put stones around the circumference of the fire.) Roast marshmallows. Throw wrapped candy all over the backyard and challenge the kids to pick up a leaf for every piece of candy they retrieve. Choose a special tree and name it. Thank God for that and pay attention to it all year. Measure and record its circumference. Estimate its height. Save a twig to compare to another next spring. Serve apple cider, spiced apple rings, or baked apples. (Let the kids help make them!)

- Try these smoked leaf prints. Spread a thin layer of petroleum jelly on one side of a glass soda bottle. Fill the bottle with cold water and hammer the cap back down. Light a candle and roll the bottle's petroleum jelly side over the flame to get a good layer of black carbon. (The cold water insulates your hand!) Now take a small leaf or other flexible object and lay it on the carbon. Press gently. Remove it carefully and transfer it, carbon side up, to a sheet of newspaper. Place typing paper over it and rub your fingers gently and completely over the leaf, transferring the carbon to the paper. Peel the leaf away.

- Play a rigorous game of volleyball in the backyard for the last time. Then take the net down for the season.

✔ Mail different leaves to a missionary living in a tropical country like Indonesia or Mexico. They will enjoy the smell even if the leaves get crushed.

The Bible says, "He has made *everything* beautiful in *its* time" (Ecclesiastes 3:11, emphasis added). Substitute your name for "everything." Thank God for making you exactly as He wanted you to be. Thank Him for aging you in His grace.

Go in Peace

All Hallow's Eve: God Promises Love to "Generations of Those Who Love Me"

Stop and Think

Framed portraits of people long dead covered the wall. There sat Grandma as a young woman in a long black skirt, her white blouse showing a row of tiny buttons. Beside her, laughing into the camera, is her sister, my great-aunt Laura. My other grandma stands behind her parents with the serene smile of the eldest. The young girl in white lace with roses in her hair takes a prim pose. She will one day become my husband's grandmother. In a frame nearby is my great-great-uncle Fred sporting a jaunty pose. They say he was debonair as a young man and a flirt even when he was old. All of the 19 people on that wall have one thing in common besides being related to me. They are all in heaven.

We were still in Hong Kong, packing for our return to the States. All these pictures fell down once when a typhoon blew in the living room wall. But they'd been repaired, and now they were carefully wrapped for shipping. I had deliberately left a long chip in one frame because the typhoon story is exciting to tell. The Chinese man helping us pack held the cracked frame out to me with some trepidation. "I not break this."

"Die fung choy," I said making sweeping motions with my arms and pointing to the picture in his hands. "Typhoon blows."

"Hi," he said. "Is." Then he pointed to all the pictures he'd wrapped. "Ancestors."

"Hi," I answered. "Is." Ancestors are so important to Chinese people that they gather at the graves of their relatives twice a year to care for the sites. They also offer various foods and miniature houses, clothes, money, and even cars made of sticks and tissue paper. These gifts are then burned so the ancestor's ghost will have the necessary supplies in his or her spirit world.

Every year Chinese people celebrate the Feast of Hungry Ghosts where these miniature items, apples, or oranges are put out for the ghosts who have no one on earth to care for them. In this way, these hungry ghosts will be content and deal more kindly with the neighborhood.

The first time we watched this celebration, I was reminded of the origins of Halloween. This tradition began in England where food was left out to fend off the hungry beggars and ghosts for the year. Like the gargoyles on Chinese temples, the English added grotesque figures to frighten any evil ghosts away.

The pictures of my ancestors were double-sealed by the packer who valued them as highly as I did, though my reasons are quite different. I value my ancestors because I know that they have passed on a legacy to me. By their faithfulness to God and their regular practice of church worship, Scripture reading, and Christian schooling, I have inherited my knowledge of the Lord from them. There was never a time I didn't know the Lover of my soul.

My family members, past and present, line the wall in my bedroom as witnesses to the promise God made thousands of years ago. He promised to be faithful to generations upon generations of people who love Him. I look forward to meeting every one of these people, some for the first time. I will thank them and Jesus for their gift of faith.

Look and Listen

Moses told of God's long-term love to families in Deuteronomy 7:9. We know his words were taught to the faithful because Jesus' mother includes them in her song (Luke 1:50). God keeps His promise of love to us every day. Some families come from a long line of knowing God's love, while other families are becoming the first in a long line to come.

Genealogies, or family trees, are listed in several places in the Bible. Jesus' line is listed twice, once in Matthew 1 and again in Luke 3. If you look in both lists, you may recognize some of Jesus' ancestors, such as Hezekiah, Solomon, King David, Boaz, Judah, Jacob, Isaac, Abraham, Noah, Methuselah, and Adam. Each has a story demonstrating God's determined love—a love that extended into a two-way relationship.

Christian speakers often tell of people who come to Christ after years of faithful prayer by their parents and grandparents. I remember a man who said his father called him to his deathbed to wish him farewell. "He told me that he'd never see me again," the speaker said with a catch to his voice, "because I refused to believe in Jesus as my Savior. My dad told me good-bye that day with tears running down his face." The speaker had to pause to compose himself. He continued, "But my dad will see me because God did answer his prayers for me. I do believe that Jesus is the Way, the Truth, and the Life. God answers prayer."

God sighting. Who prays for you? Phone your grandparents and ask them what they ask of God for you. (If they don't mention the relationship with Jesus, ask them about it.)

Proceed with Care

✔ Begin praying for a faithful relationship between your child's future spouse and God. Pray for this every so often so that by your child's dating years, he or she will know how much you value this quality in a prospective spouse.

✔ Put your family tree into your Bible. Share pictures and stories if you have them. If not, get them! Write up various questions that will elicit stories like: Tell me about your Christmas memories. What was your most joyful time? When were things really bleak? What was church worship like when you were a kid? What have you learned that is important? When the kids see your picture, what do you want them to know about you? Record the answers. (Make video- or audiotapes of the kids while you're at it!)

✔ Many families celebrate the lives of noted Christians, such as Francis of Assisi, Brother Lawrence, Martin Luther, David Livingstone, John Neumann, Amy Carmichael, and Jim Elliot. It's good to remember what the love of God can enable people to do in our world. We all draw from the same Source. Study some of the lives of noteworthy Christians. Buy books and tapes from Christian bookstores.

✔ Make apple dolls. Carve a peeled apple into a face shape. Let it set to dry. It will shrivel into a wrinkled old face.

Add black beads for eyes and a small bit of felt for a mouth. Dress it with wispy hair and a hat. Poke a hanger in the top and give it to a grandparent for a Christmas tree ornament.

✔ Make door hangers to give as treats for Halloween. As your child receives a treat, he or she can give one as well.

✔ Write out what your family believes: Who is Jesus? What did He do? How do I talk to God? How does God feel about me? Write or draw the answers on paper. Then nail this to a block of wood. Let the kids do the hammering. Add a hanger and put it on the front door. Martin Luther nailed his 95 theses to the church door on October 31.

✔ In Belgium, people eat "soul cakes" on All Hallow's Eve. The round cakes were given to beggars on that day in exchange for their promise to pray for the members of the family. A devout cook decided to invent something that would remind the beggars of eternity with each bite—thus the doughnut! Eat some doughnuts together!

✔ Most of our hymns and prayers were written by saints. Talk to your church music director about a favorite hymn writer's life. Then have a songfest.

Ask the children to think about the future. Do they see themselves all grown up? What would they look like? What would they do? What would they want to do with their grandkids? Now ask them which of those things they've already done with their own grandparents. Praise God for these wonderful experiences.

Thanksgiving Day: God Gives Us Bounty

There were unique difficulties being a missionary in a land where people counted their wealth in pigs. In the tropical heat of New Guinea, life was never simple for a mother with a baby and other small children.

Once again, the mission plane hadn't arrived on schedule. The "silver bird" still captured the attention of the natives as it brought strange foods and gadgets to the missionaries. The woman scanned the skies wondering what red tape caused the delay this time. She had enough food for one more month, but each passing day made her uneasy. Fortunately the baby drank only canned milk, and she could eat a little less so the others could have more.

After two weeks went by, the woman's husband also became concerned. Rumors of warring tribes in the north made him wonder if somehow the plane was down and the pilot was injured.

By the end of the third week, the missionary decided he would go to the nearest radio center for information and food since now their provisions were low. As she waved good-bye to her husband, the woman breathed a prayer for his safety. Then she returned to their house to count cans. If she were careful, she would have enough left for a week. It was too early to dig up her sweet potatoes, so she took the children out with her to look for other roots. She cooked into a paste whatever they found.

Each day she waited for her husband's cheery "Halooo," but he didn't come. She looked at her shelf one morning to recount the three cans of milk that remained. "Lord," she prayed, "You said You would always supply us with what we need. The baby needs milk, and I'm worried. Please help me to trust that You will provide."

The next day one of the children ran inside. "Mother! Mother! There's a native outside with three children. One is a baby, and it looks sick!"

The missionary wife hurried outside. She spoke with the native woman and learned that the woman's husband was in the mission hospital. On the way to take care of him, she'd become ill herself and had lost her ability to nurse her baby. Would the Christian lady please share milk with her?

The lady saw the native child's desperate need but thought too of her own baby. "What would you have me do, God?" she prayed.

Look and Listen

Read Matthew 6 and 1 Timothy 6:17–19. Did you ever read about the bird who held up a bank because it had no money to buy food? No? How do birds eat? (God feeds them.) Did you see the newspaper article on the trembling flower, worried that soon all its petals would be gone? No? Where does a flower get its "clothes"? What does Jesus declare will be true for people who concern themselves with whatever task God is calling them to do (Matthew 6:33)?

God grants wealth to some of His Christians—even beyond what we need to keep our bodies protected and our stomachs healthy. Some of us have more than one room to live in! Some of us have books that we own! Some of us even have more than one car! More than half of the people of the world are not wealthy. That doesn't mean we're better; it means we have been given an opportunity to be generous to others. When we are generous in this way, what does God say we are doing (1 Timothy 6:19)?

What is this heavenly treasure? Someone once asked, "If you had in heaven only what you've given away, would you have enough to live on?" Maybe this treasure is a generous nature. All we know for sure is that we need not worry about our physical needs because God has promised to provide us with what we need to survive and spread the Good News.

When God gives us even more than we need, we have the opportunity to share this heavenly treasure. God is so bountiful, He fills our cups to overflowing with His blessings. Every day could easily be Thanksgiving because every day we are given so much.

The lady missionary, by the way, gave the native woman two cans of milk. Her husband arrived home later in the day with their full shipment. The missionary woman could now provide a personal example of God's overflowing abundance.

God sighting. Before you go to sleep, thank God for specific happenings in your day. When you count your blessings like this, you will be amazed at the sheer volume of God's gifts! By recounting our blessings, we become confident that God will always provide enough to spare and enough to share!

✔ Place two corn kernels on each empty plate at your Thanksgiving feast table. Invite each person to prayerfully review the past year and decide which two events God has given him or her to share in the prayer of thanksgiving. Pass a basket around the table to receive everyone's corn kernels as you pray together. Decorate your basket together before Thanksgiving Day.

✔ Challenge the family to do an A–Z thanks. Start with blessings that start with A—apple pie, addition, or aspirin, and see if you can name one blessing from God for each letter of the alphabet. Try to make the blessings specific to your family.

✔ Ponder this: For what might you thank God that has *not* been given to you this year?

✔ Make a special cornucopia out of a grocery bag. Have the children draw and cut the various fruits listed below. Each fruit stands for the types of people God has put in our lives. As you put the cornucopia together, write your thank-You prayer on each fruit drawing.

apple—teachers, both school and Sunday school

watermelon—park keepers

grapes—people who care for the communion ware and other church worship materials

orange—truck drivers who transport food to the grocery store

lemon—refuse workers who put up with the sour so that our homes may be clean

banana—health care workers who look after us when we slip up

blueberry—city or county workers who make sure fresh, clean water gets to our homes

Make a turkey centerpiece for your feast table. Cut 6″ circles out of colored construction paper. Cut out magazine pictures that represent categories like food, clothing, shelter, friends, relatives, toys, creation's beauty, or vacations. Glue those pictures to the colored circles. Then fold the circles in half and slit them about two inches toward the center as illustrated. Cut a 6″ cardboard circle for a base. Slide the slit circles on the base and spread them so that their edges touch. Add a cut-out drawing of a turkey head. This is truly a Thanksgiving turkey!

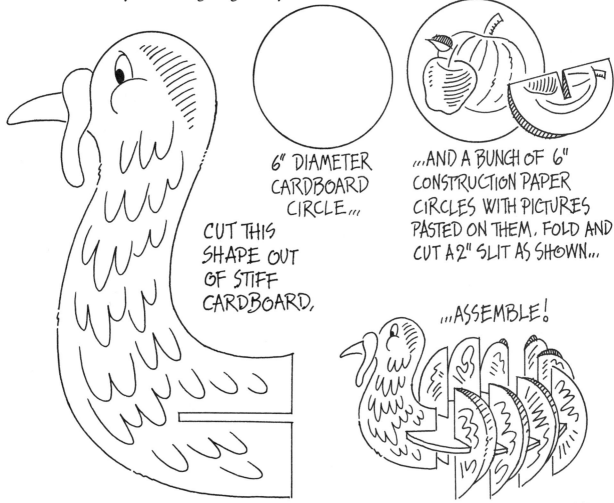

6″ DIAMETER CARDBOARD CIRCLE...

CUT THIS SHAPE OUT OF STIFF CARDBOARD,

...AND A BUNCH OF 6″ CONSTRUCTION PAPER CIRCLES WITH PICTURES PASTED ON THEM. FOLD AND CUT A 2″ SLIT AS SHOWN...

...ASSEMBLE!

- Hide a ticking kitchen timer somewhere in the house. See who can find it before it rings. The person who finds it gets to be the next one to hide it.

- Have a taste test. Blindfold the children and see who can distinguish between lemonade, orange juice, and grape juice with their noses held shut. Finally, blindfold Mom and Dad and see who can feel the difference between an apple and an orange with a bare foot. Thank God for our senses!

Line up all the shoes in your house, even the summer ones. Shoes show us where we have been. Talk about where your family has been this year. Then use your discussion as a prayer starter, thanking God for all the wonderful places He has shown you this year.

Go in Peace

Advent:
God Prepares Us for Jesus

Mary prepared the swaddling strips for her soon-to-be-born son. She poked her needle into the cloth. These cloths will cuddle the Messiah, she thought in renewed wonder. What will He look like? A quiet young woman by nature, Mary had become even more reflective.

"So many things have happened. Who would ever guess that my engagement to Joseph would not only put me in King David's line but that I would be chosen to be the mother of my Lord!" She recalled the incredible visit of the angel Gabriel, who first told her that God was coming. Then

Stop and Think

Joseph also saw an angel who told him the same news. "His name is Jesus," she mused. "The angel told each of us that."

Mary got up slowly to stretch her legs a bit. She waddled over to the open window. She'd walked down that road a few months ago to visit her cousin Elizabeth. The angel had said Elizabeth was with child. That seemed impossible at Elizabeth's age, but impossible births seemed to be in God's plan. "Already God has sent Jesus' forerunner into the world—like the herald before a king."

A Roman soldier rode by on his horse. He'd arrived with the proclamation that set Joseph packing a few days ago. God uses our enemies to do His will, thought Mary. Like many devout Jews, Mary knew that Bethlehem was foretold as the birthplace of the Messiah. She'd wondered about that with Zechariah and Elizabeth. "I live in Nazareth. How will we end up in Bethlehem?"

Mary smiled to herself. Trust God to work out the details. The Romans had ridden in last week saying everyone had to return to their birthplaces to register for a census. Joseph had been born in Bethlehem.

Mary returned to her sewing. The cloth was nearly finished. "Am I ready for You?" Mary said softly. "What do I even know about being a mother, let alone *Your* mother?" She stopped sewing a moment, thinking.

"Yes, it's true. You prepare each step before I take it, God. When Joseph would have broken the engagement, You sent the angel with a message. As I wondered where Jesus would be born, You sent the Roman soldier. Who else will You send to help me follow the path You set out for me, O Mighty One?"

God prepared several people for Jesus' birth. Zechariah's story is in Luke 1:5–25. Simeon and Anna's stories are in Luke 2:25–38. The Wise Men and the shepherds were in the right places at the right time. Even the inn was set to be overcrowded that night. The star was up. The angels were in place over the hill. God is like a director rubbing His hands in anticipation—lights! camera! action!

What about you? How does God get you ready for Jesus' birthday? Does He touch your heart as you sit in the dark, gazing at the lights on the Christmas tree? Does God turn your thoughts to His love as you sing carols to the delighted faces of old and new acquaintances? Do you catch some of God's joy when you wrap a present for Mommy or Daddy?

In December, many worship services will include Bible readings about when Jesus returns to earth. As He ascended to heaven, Jesus said that He will come back. How is God getting you ready for that day?

The Advent season is one way God prepares our hearts for Jesus. Jesus' mother knew the Messiah would come. She knew because she believed God's Word. During Advent, we remember that God keeps His word. What if this Christmas, Jesus comes to us with His angels? Are you ready to go with Him?

God sighting. What Christmas decorations do you put on your tree that God can use to draw you and your family to Him?

Proceed with Care

✔ Make ornaments by rolling out clay and cutting it with holiday cookie cutters. Poke a hole in the top of the ornament. You can also make salt dough: Combine 2 cups flour, 1 cup salt, and 3/4 to 1 cup water. Knead the mix-

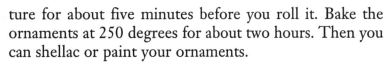

ture for about five minutes before you roll it. Bake the ornaments at 250 degrees for about two hours. Then you can shellac or paint your ornaments.

✔ Make the two cardboard tree shapes as illustrated. Slip them into each other to make a four-sided tree. Number some tags from 1 to 24, decorate them, and hang them on the cardboard tree. Each number will match an activity or treat you've prepared in advance. Starting December 1, have the children choose a number to get a surprise!

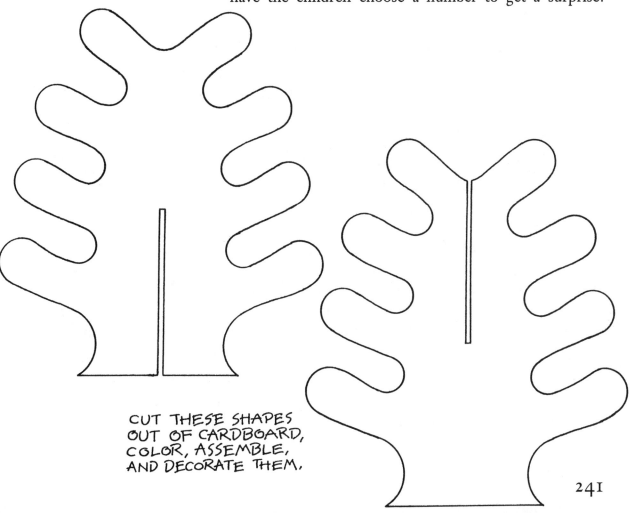

CUT THESE SHAPES
OUT OF CARDBOARD,
COLOR, ASSEMBLE,
AND DECORATE THEM.

Here are some activity/treat ideas (activity Christmas books, such as *Make a Christmas Memory*, CPH, 1996, have more ideas):

1. Dress up like angels and sing "Joy to the World."
2. Use the nativity pieces to act out the story of Jesus' birth.
3. Call Grandma and sing carols to her.
4. Pop popcorn as a birthday party favor for the birds.
5. Make homemade Christmas cards for friends.
6. Read Luke 2.
7. Decide on an anonymous gift from the family to someone else.

✔ Teach the children to embroider. Cross-stitch is probably the easiest stitch to learn. You can draw a star or a Christmas tree on gingham and then use two strands of embroidery floss to fill it in. You can also teach them the less difficult stitches to make, such as french knots and daisies. Use the embroidered cloths as gift wrap.

✔ Turn off all the lights and light some candles. Put on Christmas music like Handel's *Messiah*. Pretend you are shepherds surrounded by the angels.

✔ Many families have an Advent wreath. The wreath holds four candles, each representing a different blessing: peace, hope, joy, and love. You can make your own wreath with a Styrofoam base and greens. Or draw and decorate an Advent wreath. Cut the drawing out and glue it to a paper place mat. Use a different set of place mats for each week of Advent. The first set would have a single candle and the word *peace* stenciled on the bottom. The second set would have two candles and *hope* printed on them. The third week is joy, and the last week, love.

✔ Remember December 6 is St. Nicholas' Day. Some families like to do all their Santa activities on this day so that Christmas remains Jesus' day. Have the children decorate felt stockings while you tell them the story of St. Nicholas.

Say or sing this Advent hymn:

> Lift up your heads, you mighty gates!
> Behold, the King of glory waits.
> The King of kings is drawing near,
> The Savior of the world is here.
> He brings salvation down to earth.
> Greet Him with shouts of holy mirth.
> Our highest praise we bring,
> Our God, Creator, King.

Lutheran Worship, 24

Go in Peace

First Day of Winter: God Transforms Creation

Stop and Think

Siu Lin stared wide-eyed at his new American home. He'd spent half of his seven years in a Hong Kong refugee center until a Chicago church had agreed to sponsor his family. Now they stood, the three of them, before a huge, yellow house. Siu Lin wanted to pull away from Mother and explore, but a look from his father held him still.

The American man shook hands with Father, and the American woman gave Mother a loaf of French bread. Siu Lin felt his heart flutter like a bird about to fly. The door opened into a large kitchen with a tile floor. Siu Lin broke away from his parents and raced all through the house, room after room.

At the end of an exhausting day, Mother and Father pulled the mattress off the bed, and the three of them slept on the floor as they'd always done. Just before Siu Lin fell asleep, he heard Mother quietly weeping for little Lee Mien who'd died on the boat out of Vietnam. "Where is she now?" Mother asked Father. Since that terrible day, Siu Lin had often fallen asleep to the sound of Mother's quiet grief.

The next day, the two Americans returned with others. Mother soon got used to the grocery store; she missed the open-air market of her homeland. Father went with an American man to learn to work at a dry cleaner plant. A teacher came every day to help Siu Lin learn to improve his English and to teach him to read. She showed him books about many things. One day they went for a walk, and Siu Lin asked about the trees. "All the trees here are dying. Every day is colder. What will happen when all the leaves go?"

The teacher smiled and said in this part of the world the plants and trees closed themselves in to prepare for a winter rest.

"What is winter?" Siu Lin asked.

"Winter is a time when the earth is tilted away from the sun so it is colder. There is snow."

Siu Lin wondered about this but tucked it away for later.

"Later" arrived one incredible morning in late November. Siu Lin woke up before Mother and Father because the light felt different somehow. He looked over to the window and gasped. He carefully stepped on the cold floor and tiptoed to the window. The window looked like diamonds had flattened themselves completely across it. Siu Lin reached up to touch them but pulled his finger back from the icy coldness.

Staring through the magic window, Siu Lin could hardly breathe. Everything was covered with white flakes! They were falling out of the sky! "Mother! Father! Our house has flown to somewhere else in the night! Wake up and see!"

The three crowded around the frosted window and peered at the transformed landscape. Then hand in hand, they went to the front door. Snow wet their bare feet as they gingerly stepped into it. Feathery flakes melted on Siu Lin's pajama sleeve. He stuck his tongue out to catch some. Then he looked at Father's face and saw that snow stuck to his eyebrows and eyelashes. Siu Lin started to laugh and so did his parents. He twirled round and round with his arms out, and Mother laughed some more.

This is an amazing place, Siu Lin thought. It is a good place because it is beautiful and my mother laughs here.

Look and Listen

God shows us His designs in creation. There are patterns everywhere if you look carefully. In the four seasons we can see the pattern of our lives. Spring is like birth and childhood. Summer is compared to the vigorous years of maturing. Fall reminds us of our older years of wisdom and complex beauty. People often compare winter to dying.

God understands how we think of death as an ending. Read Philippians 3:20–21. What will we be like when we die? What does a glorious body look like? What can it do? We don't know much about what our heavenly bodies will look like. We do know that the disciples recognized Jesus when He wanted them to. He ate with them. He could appear in a closed room. And He could move up in the air.

God sighting. Think about what God shows us with water. It can be a frozen icicle for us to hold. It can be liquid, flowing all around us in a swimming pool. It can be invisible in the air, making our skin wet when there is high humidity. We know God can transform the molecules of hydrogen and oxygen into water. Imagine what He can do with our molecules. Think of it!

Proceed with Care

- ✔ Make snow ice cream: Mix 2 eggs, ½ cup sugar, 1 teaspoon vanilla, ½ cup cream. Add a big bowl of clean snow. Enjoy!

- ✔ Have a big person mark a trail through the snow. Loop around; go over, under, and around things. Then see if the rest of the family can follow the trail.

- ✔ Wad up paper like snowballs. Stand 5 to 10 feet away from the table. Turn your backs. How many "snowballs" can you toss back and up to land on the table?

- ✔ Write secret messages with lemon juice on paper. The words will magically appear when you hold them over a bare light bulb. Be careful!

- ✔ Play with artificial snow in the bathtub. Spread shaving cream on the side of the tub and draw in it with a craft stick or pile it into drifts for small toy people to play in.

- ✔ Fold a square of paper in half to get a triangle. Now fold the triangle into thirds. Cut wedges and shapes out of the edges while it is folded. Carefully unfold it to get a six-pointed snowflake. Use white thread to hang the snowflakes from the ceiling.

- ✔ Transform last year's Christmas cards into snow scenes. Use cotton swabs to put glue on the cards. Sprinkle the glue spots with sugar or silver glitter.

Read these words of 1 John 3:2 together:

Dear friends, now we are children of God, and what we will be has not yet been made known. But we know that when He appears, we shall be like Him, for we shall see Him as He is.

Use these thoughts as your prayer starter.

Christmas Day:
God Gives Us His Son as Savior

Stop and Think

The music from the Hallmark commercial died down. A man announced, "When you care enough to send the very best."

"That sure makes a good Christmas motto," said Mr. Martin. He took his arm from around Mom to point the remote at the television. The picture disappeared.

"It's bedtime, Bumpkins." Two-year-old Tootie was sleeping with her thumb in her mouth. Dad picked her up tenderly. "This one's going to be easy." He winked at Mom, and she smiled.

"Okay, Kelly. Up we go!" Mrs. Martin pulled Kelly by the feet. Kelly giggled. "I'm sending the very best to bed! Come on, hop to."

Kelly went through her familiar bedtime routine with ease. As Mom helped her into her pajamas, she asked again how many days until Christmas. "Only two more," answered Mom, tucking her under the covers.

Kelly and Mom talked to Jesus about the day. Then Daddy came in for a kiss. The lights went off, and Kelly turned on her side.

When you care enough, send the very best, she thought. I still don't have a present for Jesus yet. If I gave Him my very best, what would that be?

She thought of her teddy bear from Grandma. Teddy used to travel everywhere with Kelly. Now Teddy mostly stayed on her bed to watch her sleep. "I still love you, Teddy," Kelly whispered, cuddling her old friend. She kissed his furry cheek. "Are you my very best?"

Kelly thought of presents she'd gotten. The red 10-speed bike on her birthday crowned that day. The sleek tires and shiny gears on the new bike definitely outclassed her old bike. She remembered flying down the street last summer. "Is the bike my very best?"

"Very best, very best," drummed in Kelly's head. Daddy said those words to her just before the Christmas program. Kelly had several lines as the angel Gabriel, and she felt nervous.

Daddy said, "Just do your very best, Kelly, and it will be wonderful." Kelly wondered if sending your very best might be *doing* something rather than giving an object.

"What am I best at doing?" Kelly whispered to Teddy. She waited for him to answer. It took awhile. "Yes, that's true. I am probably the best scientist in my class." She glanced over at her Scientist of the Month certificate on the wall, but it was too dark to see the words. "How do you give to Jesus by doing a science experiment?" With this puzzling question in her mind, Kelly fell asleep.

At breakfast, Kelly asked her mom, "If I wanted to show Jesus how much I care about Him, then I'd send Him my very best. So what is my very best?"

Look and Listen

People are infinitely precious to God. He gave us a beautiful world to explore. He made the butterflies and rustling trees. His clouds change daily, and He puts a pallet of colors below our feet every day. But these things aren't His very best.

Because we are so precious, God talked to people from the very first. He spoke with Adam and Eve even after they disobeyed His only rule. He spoke to Methuselah. He talked to Noah. He often had conversations with Abraham. He talks to us every day through the Holy Spirit and the Word. But marvelous though this is, it is still not God's very best.

God knew from the beginning what He would send as His very best. He told Adam and Eve about it in Genesis 3:15. He said it again to Abraham in Genesis 12:3. Because God cared enough, He sent Jesus, His only Son. God let Mary hold His best in her arms. Others touched His tiny fingers too—a shepherd, a scholar from the East, an old man and woman. Rich or poor, male or female, Jew or Gentile, Jesus was sent as a gift to all.

God sighting. That first Christmas, God gave us His best gift. The gift of Jesus makes even more gifts from God possible, like the gift of wisdom, peace beyond understanding, and faith. Look at a Christmas scene that shows the nativity while you spend some quiet time with God. Share what happened during that time with God.

✔ Help the children understand that service is a precious gift. Draw "time" coupons, such as "I'll make your bed"; "I'll do your turn at dishes"; "I'll help you shovel"; or "I'll make breakfast." Wrap these "gifts" and place them under the tree.

✔ Sing every evening during the 12 days of Christmas. As you sing, light a German Candlemas. If you don't have one of these wood and candle sculptures, you can make one. Photocopy the pattern on the next page and use it to cut a circle from tagboard. Cut three of the six sections so they look like little doors. Use a hole punch to make holes around the edge of the circle Overlap the two triangles as indicated and glue. Place this cone on top of a knitting needle. Secure the base in a large cork or wooden block. Photocopy this page and cut out the ornaments. Make others of your choice. Use ornament hooks to hang them around the edge of the cone. Work out the balance. Place the sculpture over a radiator or other heat source and watch it spin.

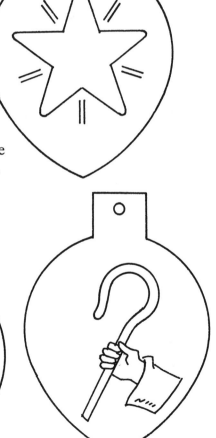

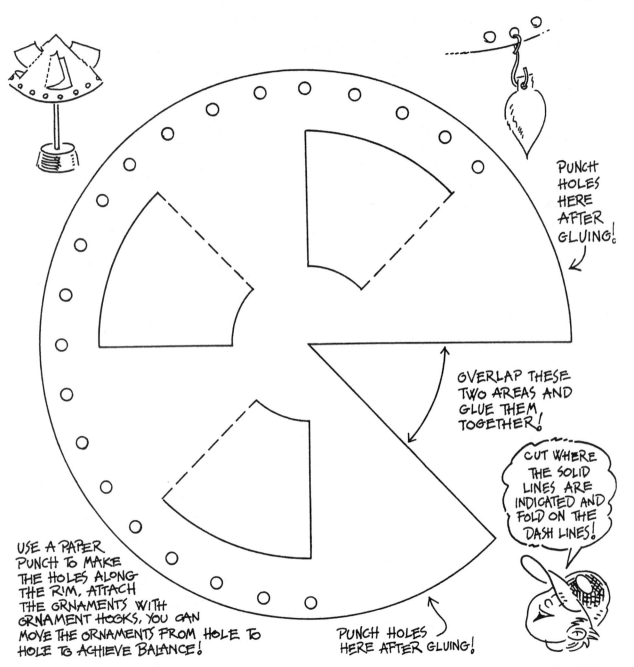

✔ Make a gift for the birds. Mix any of the following with peanut butter or suet as the glue: sunflower seeds, nuts, dry dog or cat food, raisins, dry unsweetened cereal, or dry corn. Mix by hand and flatten into bird cookies.

✔ Draw nativity characters or objects on paper and pin them to each other's shirt backs (inn, manger, Mary, Joseph, baby Jesus, donkey, shepherd, angel, sheep). Talk to each other as if the other person were actually what is on his or her piece of paper. After a few minutes let everyone try to guess who or what each person is.

✔ Make luminaries together. Fold down the top of paper lunch sacks so there's a secure top edge. Fill them with enough sand so that the votive candle you set in the center will stay in place. Line the sidewalk with them and light them at dusk. They make a lovely backdrop for singing "Silent Night."

✔ Cut up Christmas cards to make dandy puzzles for church bags!

Use a bright light to cast a shadow of your child's head. Tape paper to the wall and trace the silhouette. Repeat for other family members. Line up the drawings. These are the people God cares about so much that He sent His only Son, Jesus, to die for their sins. Use this thought as your prayer starter for each member of your family.

"Lord God, we praise You for loving our *Kelly* like You do … "

Go in Peace